An Introduction to

Intel Assembly Language

to accompany

The Essentials of Computer Organization and Architecture

Second Edition

Linda Null
Pennsylvania State University

and

Julia Lobur
Pennsylvania State University

JONES AND BARTLETT PUBLISHERS
Sudbury, Massachusetts
BOSTON   TORONTO   LONDON   SINGAPORE

World Headquarters

Jones and Bartlett Publishers
40 Tall Pine Drive
Sudbury, MA 01776
978-443-5000
info@jbpub.com
www.jbpub.com

Jones and Bartlett Publishers
Canada
6339 Ormindale Way
Mississauga, Ontario L5V 1J2
CANADA

Jones and Bartlett Publishers
International
Barb House, Barb Mews
London W6 7PA
UK

Jones and Bartlett's books and products are available through most bookstores and online book-sellers. To contact Jones and Bartlett Publishers directly, call 800-832-0034, fax 978-443-8000, or visit our website www.jbpub.com.

Substantial discounts on bulk quantities of Jones and Bartlett's publications are available to corporations, professional associations, and other qualified organizations. For details and specific discount information, contact the special sales department at Jones and Bartlett via the above contact information or send an email to specialsales@jbpub.com.

6048

ISBN-13: 978-0-7637-3585-2
ISBN-10: 0-7637-3585-X

Acquisitions Editor: Tim Anderson
Production Director: Amy Rose
Editorial Assistant: Kate Koch
Marketing Manager: Andrea DeFronzo
Manufacturing and Inventory Coordinator: Amy Bacus
Composition: Northeast Compositors
Printing and Binding: Odyssey Press, Inc.

Printed in the United States of America
10 09 08 07 06   10 9 8 7 6 5 4 3 2 1

Contents

Chapter 1

Introduction

Why should you be interested in learning assembly language? For one thing, it allows you to become very familiar with the organization and operation of your computer. Eventually, this can make you a better high-level language (HLL) programmer. In addition, a well-written assembly language program executes faster and utilizes resources more efficiently than the corresponding HLL program. This happens in part because the programmer has specific control over reading/writing memory locations as well as I/O ports. HLL subprograms can be written in assembly language to run more efficiently or to perform functions not possible in the HLL language itself.

With today's super fast CPUs, many programmers are not as concerned about writing "fast" code, since the speed of the CPU often covers up poor coding habits. In those instances in which the CPU speed cannot make up for poorly written software, many programmers don't know how to deal with the problem. Data structures and algorithms studies direct us to select appropriate data structures and efficient algorithms to help remedy the situation. However, we cannot stop there. To write software that executes efficiently, programmers must understand the underlying hardware and write code based on that knowledge. Assembly language forces programmers to understand the relationship between the hardware and each instruction they use. In addition, since all compilers translate HLL source code into machine code, knowledge of assembly language allows a programmer to associate HLL constructs with the machine language instructions that the compiler creates.

Programming in assembly is not an easy task. Even though most instruction sets are limited in number (learning 30–35 instructions is typically sufficient to write most applications), programmers are working at a much lower level, which requires them to specifically implement many of the constructs we take for granted in high level languages (such as while loops, if/else statements, etc.). An algorithm that you understand and can easily code in a high-level language may become an exercise in frustration when you attempt to code it in assembly. However, once you have mastered basic assembly language programming, even if you never write another assembly language program, understanding the low-level implementation of high-level language instructions will allow you to efficiently select and implement good algorithms for a specific architecture, resulting in efficient code.

Chapter 2

The Intel Architecture

As previously mentioned, writing an assembly language program requires a programmer to possess a good understanding of the architecture in addition to understanding the details of the instruction set for that architecture. This is because in assembly language, the programmer is responsible for more of the low-level details. For example, in a high-level language, you might find a statement such as C = A + B. However, in assembly language, the programmer must use the registers and data path to load either one or both of A and B from memory, perform the addition, and then explicitly store the result in memory location C. We have seen this in Chapters 4 and 5 of the textbook.

Programming in Intel assembly language requires knowledge of the Intel memory layout, in addition to familiarity with the registers and instructions. All Intel machines use a segmented architecture, meaning certain blocks of memory are reserved for specific types of information (such as program code, data for a program, the program stack, etc.). A **segment** is simply a special 64K-byte area that is explicitly defined to hold certain information. Intel assembly language programs are organized as a collection of these segments. Although we are familiar with referring to memory addresses as binary or hex values, we shall see shortly that Intel's use of segments allows us to refer to memory addresses as **segment:offset** pairs. One segment holds the program code; to reference an instruction, the segment and offset for the instruction within this segment are used. Another segment holds the program data; any data the program uses is located by specifying a data segment:offset pair. A third segment holds the stack. A **stack** is a Last-In-First-Out (LIFO) structure that helps to manage and manipulate data. (See Appendix A of your textbook for more information on stacks.) It stores information necessary for the program to run. For example, when a subprogram is called, the return address is stored on the stack for later reference. Anything stored on the stack is referenced using a stack segment:offset pair. A more detailed explanation of stacks appears in Chapter 3.

In our discussions of the MARIE architecture, we had no stack, no segments, and no general purpose registers. Therefore, prior to diving into Intel assembly language instructions and their use, we must first go over the Intel architecture in detail.

2.1   Processors

Before we discuss the register set, we must first talk about the processor itself. Intel has many different processors. Often, the notation 80x86 is used to refer to the 8088, 8086, 80286, 80386, and 80486 family of processors. Following these processors, Intel introduced the Pentium, followed by the Pentium I, II, III, and Pentium Pro. These processors differ in many ways, including the number of registers, the bus size, and the amount of memory that can be addressed. For example, the 8088 has 16-bit registers with an 8-bit data bus and the ability to address 1 million bytes of memory. The 8086 uses a 16-bit bus and runs faster, but addresses the same amount of memory. The 80286 runs faster still and can address up to 16 million bytes. The 80386 has 32-bit registers and a 32-bit data bus, with an ability to address 4 billion bytes of memory. The 80486 also has 32-bit registers and a 32-bit data bus, but includes a high-speed cache and a faster clock. The Pentium has 32-bit registers with a 64-bit data bus, combined with a superscalar design and a pipelined structure. Later Pentium processors add separate paths to cache and memory, as well as other enhancements that are not critical to our understanding of assembly language programming. We note that all of these architectures are backward compatible; each successive processor simply added features and more speed, but programs that run on an 8086 processor, for example, will also run on a Pentium.

2.2   Segments

We have already stated that the 8086 can address 1 million bytes. This means 20 bits are needed to identify a unique memory location. However, the registers only hold 16 bits. To get around this problem, designers divided memory into 64K byte segments. Memory locations are identified by specifying the segment in which they are housed and the offset (16 bits) within that segment. Segments are typically defined to hold code, data, and the stack for an executing program. Special registers (discussed below) contain the beginning addresses for these segments. To access a particular memory location, only the offset within a segment is required, thus allowing us to use 16 bits to identify that location. Segments must begin at locations evenly divisible by 16 (or hex 10); these locations are referred to as **paragraph boundaries**. This means the last hex digit is always zero (in binary, the last 4 bits are always zero). To minimize storage requirements, the zeroes are not stored. In order to determine a 20-bit memory address, the segment value is multiplied by 16 (its bits are shifted left by four places) and the address of the offset is added to that value.

2.3   Registers

Each processor in the Intel family has a slightly different instruction set and register set. We present a 16-bit architecture (such as that found in the 8086) in this supplement. However, in various places throughout this document we include examples from the 32-bit architecture so the reader can see the differences that exist.

Unlike MARIE, the 8086 architecture uses a general-purpose register architecture. There are eight of these general purpose registers, and although they can be used in a variety of ways, some have very specific purposes in certain instructions. Register sizes in the 80x86 Intel architectures can be 8-bit, 16-bit, or 32-bit. We focus on 16-bit registers in this supplement. The following paragraphs discuss the processor register set, which consists of general purpose registers, segment registers, and special purpose registers.

The **general purpose registers** (GPRs) are the main registers programmers use to hold data and process information. The 16-bit registers typically used to hold data include the AX, BX, CX, and DX registers. Each of these is split into two halves and accessible separately. For example, the high-order half of AX is called the AH register; the low-order 8-bits are the AL register, as seen in Figure 2.1.

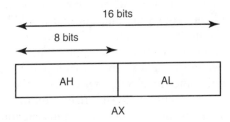

Figure 2.1 Format for General Purpose Registers

On the 80386 and higher, these registers are extended to 32-bits, and have an "E" preceding the name: EAX, EBX, ECX, and EDX. The AL, AH, AX, and EAX registers can be treated as separate registers if necessary (similarly for BX, CX, and DX).

The AX register is similar to the AC in MARIE; it is used as the primary accumulator. Many instructions, including multiply and divide, assume the use of AX implicitly (which means the contents of this register are used in the instruction and/or modified after the instruction executes). The BX register, also called the base register, can be used to extend addressing, in addition to its general-purpose applications. It is often used for indirect addressing. It can also be used in conjunction with the SI and DI registers (as discussed shortly). The general-purpose CX register, so named as it is used for counting, can be referenced implicitly in certain instructions so that the value in the CX register is incremented or decremented automatically. This is useful for looping. The DX register (for data) is implicitly referenced in many input/output operations, as well as some arithmetic operations. All of these registers can be used as general-purpose registers, but they each have special functions in certain instructions, as we will see in Chapter 4.

The general purpose registers also include **index registers**, which are used in Intel assembly language as pointers into memory. These 16-bit registers are typically used with string instructions and include the source index (SI) register and the destination index (DI) register. (There are also EDI and ESI registers on 80386s and above.) Although the SI and DI registers are generally used with strings, the BX register can be used to index strings in much the same manner. We cover SI and DI in more detail in Chapter 4 when we introduce string instructions.

Because memory is divided into segments, we must be able to identify the start of a given segment. 16-bit **segment registers** are used to store the beginning addresses for these segments. We need a code segment (CS) register, a data segment (DS) register, and a stack segment (SS) register. In addition, there is an extra segment (ES) register that provides a means to address an additional segment if necessary. (On the 80386 and later, there are two additional extra segment registers: FS and GS.) We stated earlier that segments are limited to 64K. What if your program were larger than this? You could still run your program, but you would have to store your executable code in multiple segments. We do not include examples requiring multiple code segments in this supplement.

We know that we must use a segment:offset pair to specify a memory location. For example, since the CS register contains the starting address of the program's code segment, a given offset (found in the IP register, discussed below) uniquely identifies a program instruction. The DS register contains the starting address of a program's data segment (which stores the global variables), so this address plus an offset (found in the instruction itself) references a specific byte of data in memory. The SS register helps in the implementation of a stack and allows us to retrieve (pop) and place (push) data onto the stack. This register points to the beginning of the stack, and SS:SP identifies the element on the stack to which the instruction refers (SP is explained below). Generally, you do not modify SS within the program itself. ES allows you to use an extra pointer when modifying either CS or DS might cause a problem, thus allowing two different code segment pointers or two different data segment pointers to exist at the same time. An Intel assembly language programmer must always know which segment pointer is the "default" pointer. At first glance, this might appear easy—instructions are offset from CS by default; data are offset from DS by default; and anything on the stack is offset from SS by default. However, some instructions use these registers implicitly. For example, in string instructions, the SI register specifies an offset relative to the DS, while the DI register specifies an address relative to ES. For this reason, it is a good idea to be certain about the defaults for various instructions.

In addition to general purpose registers and segment registers, there are two **stack registers**: the BP (base pointer) register and the SP (stack pointer) register. The BP register is used as a pointer to reference parameters in procedure (subprogram) calls (both addresses and data). This is done by using an SS:BP combination. The SP register points to the current word on the stack being accessed, and is combined with the SS register (SS:SP). The stack registers are often classified as **pointer registers** since they are used to point into the stack. One additional pointer register is the IP (instruction pointer) register. The IP register always uses CS (CS:IP). We provide more detail on how these registers are used in Chapter 4 when we present the instruction set.

The last register we examine is the **flags** register, which cannot be referenced directly by instructions. This register contains **status bits** that are used to determine the outcome of certain instructions involving comparisons and arithmetic changes. A single bit is tested, and the outcome of the instruction execution is dependent on that bit value. Not all of the bits in the flag register are relevant to introductory assembly language programming. Figure 2.2 depicts the bits with which a beginning programmer should be familiar.

15	14	13	12	11	10	9	8	7	6	5	4	3	2	1	0
				O	D	I	T	S	Z				P		C

Figure 2.2 Flag Register

Status bits include:

- The overflow (O) bit indicates if overflow has occurred during an arithmetic operation.
- The direction (D) flag is used by string operations to check direction (left or right).
- The interrupt (I) flag specifies whether all interrupts should be processed or ignored.
- The trap (T) flag allows the processor to be operated in debug mode (single step at a time), which is very useful for debugging programs.
- The sign (S) flag indicates the sign of the result of an arithmetic operation.
- The zero (Z) flag holds the result of an arithmetic or comparative operation (where 1 indicates a zero result).
- The parity flag (P) indicates odd or even parity.
- The carry (C) flag contains the carry from a high-order bit as the result of an arithmetic operation, or the contents of the last bit for a shift or rotate operation.

In summary, the 8086 has the following registers:

General Purpose Registers
- AX   Accumulator register: GPR used mainly for calculations and input/output
- BX   Base register: the only GPR that can be used as an index
- CX   Count register: GPR used for loop instructions
- DX   Data register: GPR used for input/output and implicit in multiply and divide

Segment Registers
- CS   Code Segment: 16-bit number that points to the start of the active Code Segment
- DS   Data Segment: 16-bit number that points to the start of the active Data Segment
- ES   Extra Segment: 16-bit number that points to the active extra segment
- SS   Stack Segment: 16-bit number that points to the start of the active Stack Segment

Pointer Registers
- IP   Instruction Pointer: 16-bit number that points to the offset of the next instruction
- SP   Stack Pointer: 16-bit number that points to the offset of the stack

- **BP**   Base Pointer: 16-bit number used to pass data to and from the stack

Index Registers
- **SI**   Source Index: used by string operations to designate the source
- **DI**   Destination Index: used by string operation to designate the destination

Flag Register (holds status bits to indicate various conditions)

2.4 Memory Organization

We explained previously how Intel architectures use a segmented memory. However, we note that the programmer has significant control over how these segments are viewed by the architecture. For example, it is possible to force the code, data, and stack segments into one, single 64K segment by using the "tiny" assembler directive (a **directive** simply tells the assembler to perform a specific task). We list some of the memory model options in Table 2.1. "Near" means "in the same segment" and "far" means "in different segments." For example, near data would be data in the same segment, whereas far data are data in a different data segment. The memory model a program uses is specified using the .MODEL directive, as we will see in sample programs following.

One more comment about memory on an Intel machine: Intel uses a little endian format (see the textbook for further information on big and little endian). The data bus can move and store 16-bits at a time (so a word is 16

Table 2.1 Memory Models

Memory Model	Code	Data	Description
tiny	near	near	code, data, and stack in one 64K segment
small	near	near	code and data in separate 64K segments
medium	far	near	data is limited to one 64K segment; code not limited
compact	near	far	code is limited to one 64K segment; data not limited
large	far	far	code and data size not limited
huge	far	far	same as large

bits). If the 16-bit word 1234h is stored at address 0h, then the byte storing 34 is located at address 0h, and the byte storing 12 is located at address 1h.

2.5   Addressing Modes

The 8086 architecture provides 17 different ways to combine addressing modes and access memory. However, there are seven main addressing modes that a programmer should be able to use. They include:

1. **Direct:** With this addressing mode, the instruction itself contains the address in memory where the operand is stored. For example, if the instruction is MOV AX,COUNT (which takes the value specified by the second operand and copies it to the location specified by the first operand), then COUNT specifies the effective address of the memory location to be moved to AX. This is also called **displacement-only addressing.** There is a variation on direct addressing called **direct-offset.** This addressing mode calculates the effective address by using arithmetic operations to modify the address. For example, MOV CX,TBL+2 would move the data two bytes from TBL into CX.

2. **Immediate:** The operand is contained within the instruction as a constant or an expression. For example, MOV AX,16 would move the value 16 into AX. This addressing mode is used only for the second operand.

3. **Register:** A register contains the operand to be used. For example, MOV AX,BX would move the value in BX to AX. Depending on the actual instruction, this mode can be used for either operand.

4. **Indirect:** In this mode, the SI, DI, BX, and BP registers are used inside square brackets to indicate a reference to memory. (Note: if coding for 386 and above, the EAX, EBX, ECX, and EDX registers can also be used.) For example, MOV AX,[BX] would use the value found in BX as the effective address of the operand in memory. The instruction MOV AX,[SI] would use the value found in SI as the effective address of the operand to move into AX. This is also called **register indirect addressing.**

5. **Base-displacement:** Like indirect addressing, this mode uses BX, BP, DI, or SI and adds a displacement to form the effective memory address. For example, MOV CX,[SI+2] uses the SI offset plus 2 as the effective address of the data to move into CX. This is also called **based relative addressing.**

6. **Base-Index:** This addressing mode forms the effective address by combining a base register (BX or BP) with an index register (SI or

DI). For example, the instruction MOV AX,[BX+DI] uses the address in BX plus the address in DI as the effective address of the data to move into AX. This is also called **based indexed addressing**.

7. **Base-Index-with-Displacement:** This addressing mode is a variation of base-index and uses a base register, an index register, and a displacement, as in the instruction MOV AX,[BX+SI+4].

All memory accesses must be done using these modes, either alone or in combination. The BX, SI, DI, and BP registers can be used to provide many interesting combinations, including:

[BX + SI]	[SI]	[BX + SI] + d8
[BX + DI]	[DI]	[BX + DI] + d8
[BP + SI]	d16	[BP + SI] + d8
[BP + DI]	[BX]	[BP + DI] + d8
[SI] + d8	[BX + SI] + d16	[SI] + d16
[DI] + d8	[BX + DI] + d16	[DI] + d16
[BP] + d8	[BP + SI] + d16	[BP] + d16
[BX] + d8	[BP + DI] + d16	[BX] + d16

where d8 and d16 are 8-bit and 16-bit positive or negative displacements, respectively. The actual displacement can be the offset of a variable or an immediate value, or both. The displacement can be inside the [ ] or outside. Each of these addressing modes has several variations. For example:

d8[BX] and [BX][d8] and [d8][BX] and [d8+BX] are all the same, as are [BX][SI]+d16 and [BX + SI + d16].

Addresses in an assembly language program can be short, near, or far. A **short address** is limited to 8 bits and must be contained in the current segment (found in the appropriate segment register). A **near address** assumes the current segment and consists of 16 bits. A **far address** is composed of both the segment and the offset, and contains 32 bits. Certain instructions, such as JMP and CALL, can use short, near, and far addresses. Most programs written by beginners are small enough so that far addresses are seldom necessary. We cover addresses and addressing modes in additional detail when discussing the instructions in Section 4.

2.6 Review Questions

1. 80x86 processors allow only a 16-bit offset, but can address 2^{20} different locations. Explain.
2. List all of the 8086 8-bit registers.

3. List all of the 8086 16-bit registers.
4. List all of the 8086 segment registers.
5. List all of the 8086 general purpose registers.
6. Can you think of a common use for each of the following address modes?
   a) register
   b) direct
   c) immediate
   d) indirect
   e) based indexed

Chapter 3

Assembly Programming Environment

Before we introduce the instruction set for the 8086, we need to explain the programming environment. It is important to understand the complete process involved in creating, assembling, running, and testing these programs. You need certain tools for this process, and we examine these tools in this section. Once you are familiar with both the instruction set and programming environment, you can begin writing programs.

3.1 Assembly Programming Process

An assembly language source code program is created using a text editor. This type of tool is widely available. Any editor that saves files in text (ASCII) format can be used. (Most assemblers require that the source files have a .ASM extension.) This .ASM file is the source code written directly by the programmer.

The second tool needed is an assembler, which translates your source code file into object code. This translation includes replacing symbolic addresses by numeric ones, replacing symbolic opcodes by machine opcodes, reserving memory storage for instructions and data, and translating constants into machine representation. The assembler allows a programmer to use mnemonics instead of zeroes and ones when writing code, in addition to providing the ability to use variables and labels. Most assemblers are two-pass assemblers, building the symbol table on the first pass, and filling it in on the second pass, thus allowing it to generate the machine code for the source program. Intel assemblers such as MASM and TASM are very popular. GNU even has a freely available assembler for Linux. There are other assemblers for Intel as well, including A86, FASM, GoASM, Gas, SpAsm, Terse, HLA, and NASM. Some are free, while others must be purchased. Some (such as MASM and TASM) work only with Windows and DOS machines, while others (such as FASM, GAS, NASM, and Terse) work on Linux and BSD machines in addition to Windows and DOS. Not all of these assemblers are compatible (a program written for one assembler may not work with another). Code in this supplement was tested using MASM and TASM. Check with your instructor to see which assembler you should use.

Once you have created your source code file and assembled it, you need a linker to generate the actual executable program code. MASM and TASM include linkers. The assembly process typically creates a file with a .OBJ extension, and, after linking, the executable file has a .EXE extension.

For example, if you are using Borland's Turbo assembler, TASM, the commands to assemble and link would be:

```
C:\>tasm filename.asm
C:\>tlink filename
```

If you are using the Microsoft assembler MASM, the commands vary depending on the version. Some versions allow you to simply type MASM, at which time you are prompted for the source code file name, the .LST file name (listing file), and the .OBJ file name. When complete, you need to use the link command to link the .OBJ file. Below, we assemble, link, and run the program prog1:

```
C:\>masm
Microsoft Macro Assembler Version X.XX
Source filename [.ASM]: prog1
Object filename [.OJB]: prog1
Source listing [NUL.LST]: prog1
Cross-reference [NUL.CRF]:
```

[messages about the assembly process occur here]

```
C:\>link
Microsoft Overlay Linker Version X.XX
Object Modules [.OBJ]: prog1+io
Run File [PROG1.EXE]:
List File [NUL.MAP]:
```

```
C:\>prog1
Enter your first number:    84
...
```

Your instructor may have created a batch file so you can assemble and link in the same step. Please check with your instructor for the specific details on your programming environment.

Regardless of which assembler you use, upper and lower case can be used interchangeably in most places in your source code. However, assembly language programs are not written in a free-format style. Instead, each statement is written one per line. Each statement has a specific format as well, and is split into the following pieces, separated by either spaces or tab characters:

Label   Opcode   Operand   Comment

The optional label value is an identifier used to symbolically represent a given memory location (which could be data, an instruction, a subprogram, etc.). Each assembler varies as to what represents a legal label. For example, some allow 32 characters, while others allow only 4. Labels are useful since they make it easy to rearrange code, add instructions, and remove instructions without having to recalculate memory addresses. In Section 3.2.1 we examine legal labels for the Intel 8086.

The opcode field value represents the actual instruction to be executed. The mnemonic value in this field may require additional information (such as one or two operands). The comment field begins with a semicolon and is used to comment the current statement or a block of code, which is very useful in explaining how a section of code actually works. Good assembly language programs include good comments.

We summarize the assembly programming process as follows:

1. Create an assembly language source code file using a text editor and save the file with a .ASM file extension.
2. Assemble the program (using your assembler of choice) to create the object file (.OBJ file extension). If there are errors, go back into the editor, modify your program, and reassemble. If there are no errors, continue.
3. Generate the executable file (.EXE file extension) by linking the object module.
4. Run your program and test thoroughly, remembering to test for special cases.
5. If you modify your source code, you must reassemble and relink.
6. DEBUG (see Section 3.3) can be used to step through your program one line at a time. This is useful for finding errors in a program's logic.

As with any programming language, when writing in assembly language it is a good idea to start early, write a little, test frequently, and save often.

3.2   Assembly Programming Elements

This section introduces various programming elements. Some are required, while others are optional. Many of these have nothing to do with a particular program per se; they are required to direct the assembler in performing certain operations.

3.2.1 Identifiers and Labels

Identifiers are names you can give to data items and actual instructions. If you have programmed before, you are familiar with the concept of a variable name. In addition, in assembly language we have labels, which are names for addresses of instructions. Both identifiers and labels are examples of symbolic names, which are subject to certain rules. For Intel assembly, these rules include: limiting the length to 31 characters; allowing letters, digits, and the symbols '@', '$', '_', and '?' to be used; and prohibiting the use of any digit as the first character in the name.

3.2.2 Literals

Programs can contain literal values as well as variables. These include numbers (binary, octal, decimal, or hexadecimal), characters (enclosed in single quotes), and strings (enclosed in single quotes). Strings require some type of termination character to denote the end of string. In 8086, we use a '$' to delimit strings.

Because numeric values can be expressed in different bases, we must let the assembler know which base to use. We do this by appending the appropriate character to the numeric value. For example, 10h would mean hexadecimal 10, while 10b would mean binary 10. An 'o' is used for octal, while a 'd' is used for decimal, which is also the default.

3.2.3 Directives

Assembly language programs consist of collections of statements. These statements can be actual assembly language instructions, or they can be **directives**. There are certain assembly directives required in each program. Consider our previous discussion of the various memory models. The programmer must specify how the segments of the program are to be treated. The **.MODEL** directive is used for this. We also know programs often use stacks. The **.STACK** directive should be declared even if the program will not use a stack. Recall that stacks are used for subprogram calling (storing the return address) and for passing parameters. They can also be used to temporarily save registers or memory contents. In addition, they are used for interrupt handling while programs are running.

A program's data segment is defined using the **.DATA** directive. The data segment allocates memory to all declared variables. There are different data allocation and initialization directives. **DB** defines a byte (allocates 8 bits); **DW** defines a word (16 bits); and **DD** defines a double word (32 bits). In addition, on the 386 and higher, **DQ** defines a quad word (64 bits) and **DT** defines ten bytes (80 bits). Each variable must be declared using one of these directives to specify how much memory to reserve. The programmer has the option of initializing these values during the allocation process. In Intel assembly, data definition directives can be followed by one single value, or multiple values separated by commas. We have several examples in the sections that follow.

An assembly language program must also have a code segment. The **.CODE** directive is used to define this segment. This is the section of your program where the actual executable code resides.

The **END** directive is used to indicate the end of your program. This tells the assembler that the program is done and that the fetch/decode/execute cycle is finished. There may be additional statements following the END statement, but they will not be assembled once END has been reached.

Every 80x86 program must have at least one procedure (any additional subprograms are defined as separate procedures). A procedure is defined by a **PROC/ENDP** statement pair. These directives are used to specify the beginning and end of a procedure. In addition, procedures should be named, with the name appearing in both the PROC and ENDP statements. For example, Hello PROC, followed by a separate Hello ENDP statement, indicates the beginning and ending of a procedure named Hello.

Once the code, data, and stack segments are defined in your program, their base addresses must be initialized. By default, programs begin with the DS and ES registers pointing to the Program Segment Prefix (PSP). The programmer must change DS so that it points to the actual program's data segment by including the following two statements:

```
mov   AX, @DATA
mov   DS, AX
```

Additional useful directives include:

1. EQU: The equate directive creates absolute symbols and aliases by assigning an expression or value to the declared variable name. The format for the equate directive is: name EQU expression. As an example, suppose your program contains: pi EQU 3.14159. The assembler will replace each occurrence of pi with the decimal value 3.14159.

2. ORG: The origin directive specifies the address where the program is to be loaded and begin execution. For example, ORG 100h indicates that the first executable statement will be loaded at address 100h. If you are creating a single segment .COM program, the ORG 100h directive must be specified.
3. TITLE: This directive allows a title to be placed at the top of each page of an assembler listing file. For example, TITLE FirstProg would print FirstProg at the top of each page.
4. PAGE: This directive can be used to specify the line length and width for a program listing, but the more common use is for generating page breaks. Any time the directive PAGE appears, the list file will contain a page break.

3.2.4 Program Structure: Putting the Pieces Together

We are now ready to look at our first Intel assembly language program, a very simple program to print "Hello world." You can use your editor of choice to type in the following assembly program. Your assembler may be sensitive to label placement, tabs, and spaces, so please consult your documentation.

```
;; This is my first program and will print Hello world
            .MODEL  SMALL
            .STACK  100h
            .DATA
Message     DB          'Hello world', 13, 10, '$'
            .CODE
First       PROC
            mov         AX, @data
            mov         DS, AX
            mov         DX, offset Message
            mov         AH, 9h      ; 9h is the code used to
                                    ; 'display string'
            int         21h         ; Standard call for I/O
            mov         AL, 0
            mov         AH, 4ch;    ; return control to operating
                                    ;  system
            int         21h
First       ENDP
            END         First       ; indicates end of program
```

Each instruction in the above program consists of an optional label field, followed by an operation field (either a directive or an opcode), followed by optional operands. The program begins with the .MODEL directive that

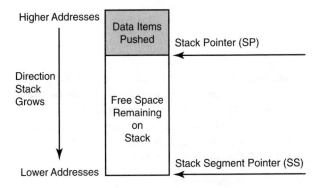

Higher Addresses

Data Items
Pushed

Stack Pointer (SP)

Direction
Stack
Grows

Free Space
Remaining
on
Stack

Lower Addresses

Stack Segment Pointer (SS)

Figure 3.1 The Stack

specifies the memory model to be used. We are using .SMALL, which is a common directive for beginning programs. The .STACK directive allows us to define a stack segment. This directive with no argument creates a stack of 1024 bytes. When items are pushed onto a stack, the stack grows downward in memory, as shown in Figure 3.1. For example, if you push the word X (2 bytes) using the instruction push X, SP is decreased by 2 and X is stored beginning at address SS:SP. SP always points to the top of the stack (or the newest item on the stack). Similarly, if you pop a word using the instruction pop Y, the word pointed to by SP is placed into Y, and SP is incremented by 2.

The .DATA directive specifies the beginning of the data segment, where variables are declared and data are stored. Variables may be initialized at this time, but initialization is not required. The only data defined in this program is a string named Message. We use the DB directive to define a string of bytes (which happens to be the message we want to print). Variables are typically defined using DB or DW, depending on whether we want the variable defined to be bytes or words. Strings are generally defined using DB, as each character requires a byte for storage. Numeric values can be either bytes or words, depending on their range of values. In addition to one single value, a sequence of values can be specified with either directive (we see a sequence of characters for the string in our program). For example:

```
OneByte    DB    4,6,8
```

declares three consecutive variables, where OneByte has a value of 4, OneByte+1 has a value of 6, and OneByte+2 has a value of 8. This is equivalent to declaring:

```
OneByte    DB    4
           DB    6
           DB    8
```

or

```
OneByte    DB    4,6
           DB    8
```

If a value will eventually be stored in a variable and the programmer does not wish to initialize that memory location, a '?' can be used to indicate this unknown value. Although the programmer does not give an initial value, *some* value is actually stored in memory at that location. When a programmer declares variables as follows, it is simply an indication that those (unknown) initial values will not be used:

```
OneByte    DB    ?    ; OneByte has no initial value
OneWord    DW    ?    ; OneWord has no initial value
```

As noted previously, our string 'Hello world' is terminated by a dollar sign. The 13 and 10 after the string but before the dollar sign are used for carriage return and line feed. In fact, many people include the following declarations in the data segment:

```
CR    EQU    13    ; carriage return
LF    EQU    10    ; line feed
```

This allows the string to be defined as follows:

```
Message    DB    'Hello world', CR, LF, '$'
```

The .CODE directive specifies the beginning of the actual code for the program. Following this, we see the name of the main procedure, First (which is associated with the PROC and ENDP directives). The statements:

```
mov    AX, @data
mov    DS, AX
```

are standard in every program and load the data segment register with the appropriate address. The statements:

```
mov    DX, offset Message
mov    AH, 9h    ; 9h is the code used to 'display string'
int    21h       ; Standard call for I/O
```

take care of moving the address of the message into a register and calling the appropriate DOS function call to display a string. The int instruction is a special way to call DOS. The system call that actually executes is dependent on the value placed in the AH register. 9h is used to display a string whose address is in the DX register, up to but not including the first dollar sign character in the string. This is why the Message string was terminated by '$'.

The statements:

```
mov    AL, 0
mov    AH, 4ch;      ; return control to operating system
int    21h
```

allow control to be returned to the operating system. Assembly programs do not simply halt, as they do in C or C++. If you do not include this code sequence in your program, the computer will continue to fetch, decode, and execute whatever it finds in the location pointed to by the program counter register (which is more than likely going to be garbage). Therefore you *must* explicitly end your program using the code segment above.

3.3   Debug

Writing assembly language programs can be difficult. This is true in part because the programmer is required to explicitly implement many structures we take for granted in higher-level languages. Debugging and tracing assembly language programs can also be frustrating. Therefore, we recommend the use of a debugger. Debugger programs can display register and memory contents as they change, and allow you to step through the program one line at a time so you can find any bugs in your program. This is *very* useful when trying to locate logic errors, or simply when attempting to understand the behavior of your program.

Debug is an interactive debugger that is supplied with both DOS and Windows. More sophisticated assembly debuggers include Microsoft CodeView and Borland Turbo Debugger. All debuggers allow you to assemble programs, view the source code and its corresponding machine code, view registers, flags, and memory contents, enter new values into memory or move values from one location to another, search for values in memory, and trace or execute programs. Since Debug is free and very simple, we cover it briefly in this supplement.

The most common Debug commands include:

Commands for program creation, execution, and debugging

A	Assemble symbolic instructions from source code into machine code
G	Run the executable program in memory within Debug itself
P	Proceed or execute a set of related instructions
R	Display or modify the contents of one or more registers
T	Trace the execution of one instruction and dump contents of all registers to screen

U   Unassemble (disassemble) machine code into symbolic code
     (mnemonic form)

Commands for memory manipulation
C   Compare two areas of memory
D   Display the contents of an area of memory
E   Enter data into memory, beginning at a specific location
F   Fill memory locations with specific values
M   Move (actually a copy) contents of memory locations
S   Search a given memory range for a specific value

Commands for input/output
I   Read one byte of data from a specified port
L   Load the contents of a disk file into memory
O   Output one byte of data to a specified port
N   Name a program
W   Write a program out to disk

Miscellaneous commands
Q   Quit the debug session
?   Display a help screen (not available in all versions of Debug)

Debug presents a very simple environment with a command line inter-
face, and, when first loaded, presents several defaults, which include the
following:

1. Programs originate at offset 0100h (which implies IP is set to 0100h).
2. Segment registers are set to point just above the debug.exe
   program.
3. 256 bytes of stack space are reserved at the end of the current
   segment.
4. Bits in the flags register are set to overflow clear, direction flag up,
   interrupts enabled, sign flag positive, zero flag clear, carry flag
   clear, and odd parity.

Debug allows you to enter your source code in addition to running your
program; however, we suggest you use a more user-friendly editor to
create your source code, and use Debug for executing and debugging your
programs.

To start debug, simply type "Debug" followed by the program name, in
a DOS prompt window:

```
C:\> Debug  MyProg.exe
```

At this time you should see a hyphen (-). This prompt indicates that Debug is ready for a command. (A command may be followed by parameters, separated by commas or spaces, as we see later.) For example, if you type:

```
-R <Enter>
```

you should see the contents of all of the registers:

```
AX=0000 BX=0000 CX=0000 DX=0000 SP=FFEE BP=0000 SI=0000 DI=0000
DS=0AF7 ES=0AF7 SS=0AF7 CS=0AF7 IP=0100 NV UP EI PL NZ NA PO NC
0AF7:0100 031F                ADD      SI,CX
```

What does all of this mean? Each register is shown with its corresponding hex value. For example, the AX, BX, CX, DX, BP, SI, and DI registers are all 0000. The stack pointer SP is FFEE, while the 4 segment registers, DS, ES, SS, and CS all contain 0AF7. IP, the instruction pointer, normally starts at 0100 since this is where the code portion of a program typically starts (as an offset from CS). The code segment:offset pair 0AF7:0100 represents the address of the next instruction and the actual value stored at that address is 13B0, which Debug believes to be the instruction to add the SI and CX registers. Since we have no real program loaded, this really doesn't mean much at this time. Please note that on your computer, the displayed values may vary from what is shown above.

The assembler uses the DS, ES, SS, and CS registers to manage instructions and data. When we create a program using Debug, on each line that we assemble we see the segment:offset pairs. For example, consider the following instruction:

```
1BC0:0104  MOV  AX, BX
```

The first number, 1BC0, corresponds to the segment in memory being used. The second value, 0104, is the offset within this segment. The MOV instruction is actually stored at this location.

You can see the contents of a specific register by using its name as a parameter with the R command:

```
-R AX
AX: 0000
:
```

The Debug prompt has changed from a hyphen to a colon. This indicates that you can change the value of that register. If you type a new value, it is placed in the register; if you simply press "Enter," the register is unchanged.

If you specify a filename when you invoke Debug, the entire file is loaded. If this is an executable (machine code) file, you can immediately run it. You can also load programs using the N and L commands. To load a program, you must first name the file. To initialize a filename, use the N command:

```
-N a:MyProg.exe
```

You can now load this file:

```
-L
```

If no address is given, the file is loaded at CS:0100h. Debug also records the number of bytes read in BX and CX.

You can enter assembly mnemonics directly into Debug using the command:

```
-A
```

Please note that you can assemble portions of your program. For example:

```
-A 100
```

will assemble at CS:100. However, we recommend that you use Debug as a debugger and *not* as an assembler (use the Debug filename option when starting Debug).

To execute a loaded program, type:

```
-G
```

If a parameter value is specified, that value acts as a breakpoint. For example:

```
-G 120
```

executes from the current location and stops before the instruction located at offset CS:120. You can also specify a range of instructions to execute. The following command starts execution at CS:100 and stops before the instructions at offset CS:120:

```
-G = 100 120
```

One very useful command is the Dump command, which dumps all bytes in a specified range. For example:

```
-D 150 15B
```

dumps all the bytes from address DS:0150 through DS:015B. Since DS is the default segment, if you want to dump from another segment location, you must specify that explicitly:

```
-D ES:150 15B
```

A memory dump shows the segment and offset address of the first bytes for each line of output. Each line of output consists of pairs of hex digits that represent the contents of each byte. The characters on the right are the ASCII representation of each byte. For example, a dump for offsets 0100h through 011Fh (with a segment register value of 1F42) might be:

```
1F42:0100: e4 08 10 a0 f0 22 26 04 14 83 10 a0 f0 22 f0 25   ....."&......".%
1F42:0100: 00 34 00 0a 00 54 00 68 00 65 00 20 00 64 00 61   .4...T.h.e. .d.a
```

Another useful command is ?, which displays a help screen. This is not available on all versions of Debug.

Although Debug is useful for running and debugging programs, if you need to edit your programs, you should use your original editor and then reassemble. Debug can be used to insert new instructions and then reassemble the program, but this is beyond the scope of this supplement.

3.4   Review Questions

1. Draw a picture illustrating the contents of memory given the following data declarations:

```
Name     DB    'Bob'
Age      DB    16
Values   DW    18,20
Stuff    DB    'E',5,'P'
Mesg     DB    'H'
         DB    'I'
```

2. What is displayed by the following segment of code containing DOS display string calls for the definitions listed below?

```
         mov    DX, offset Msg
         mov    AH, 9h
         int    21h
a. Msg   DB     'I program, therefore I am', 13, 10, '$'
b. Msg   DB     'This is a silly message$', 13, 10, '$'
c. Msg   DB     'Hi.   ', 13, 10, '$'
d. Msg   DB     'Hello world', 13, 10, '$'
```

3. Write the appropriate variable declarations and code to produce the following output:

```
Stair
    Step
        Output
```

3.5 Programming Assignments

1. Write a program to print your name and age to the screen. Label all output.
2. Write a program to print the following. Be sure you have a carriage return on the last line.

```
This is a good day
    to start programming
        in assembly language.
```

Chapter 4

80x86 Instructions

In the following sections, we review some basic instructions used by the 80x86 architecture. This is by no means a complete list of the Intel instruction set. However, the instructions we cover are sufficient for most applications. We group the instructions into several categories. In this section we cover data movement, arithmetic operations, control structures, and Boolean and bit manipulation. In Chapter 5, we cover arrays and strings.

 ## 4.1   Data Movement Instructions

Intel's 16-bit instruction set architecture provides a lean set of mnemonics for moving bytes from one location to another within the computer. Of course, when we refer to data movement in this context, what really happens is that data is copied from one storage element to another storage element, including register-to-register, memory-to-register, and register-to-memory movement. In 80x86 assembly language, you cannot move a value directly from one memory address to another. Memory-to-memory transfers must pass through at least one register.

General data movement is achieved through a single mnemonic, MOV, the format of which is:

```
MOV    <destination>, <source>
```

Execution of the MOV instruction causes a copy of the bytes in <source> to be placed in <destination>. <Source> and <destination> must be the same size. Both must be 8-bit bytes, or both must be 16-bit words; otherwise, the assembler generates an error message and the program will not assemble. We provide the format of the MOV instruction for each of the seven 8086 addressing modes.

Immediate
In the immediate addressing mode, the source operand is taken to be a literal value.

```
mov AX, 14h      ; Places 14h in register AX.
mov Total, 0     ; Moves zero to the memory
                 ;   location named Total.
```

There are two restrictions to the immediate addressing mode:

1. The largest source operand for a byte MOV is FFh, and the largest for a word MOV is FFFFh.

```
mov AL, 160h     ; Illegal!
```

2. The destination cannot be a segment register. If the need should arise to place a literal value in a segment register, the value must be first placed in one of the general registers, and then moved to the segment register.

```
mov SS, 100h     ; Illegal!
```

Direct
Direct addressing mode requires either the source or the destination operand (but not both!) to be a memory address. DS is the default segment for the memory reference, but it can be overridden.

```
mov BX, Sum          ; Places DS:Sum in BX
mov [400], AL        ; Copies AL to DS:[400]
mov CX, ES:[104]     ; Retrieves the byte at
                     ;   location 104h in the Extra
                     ;   Segment and copies it into CX.
```

As mentioned in Chapter 2, the physical location of the memory operand, its effective address, is a 20-bit address determined by the value in the explicit or implicit segment register and the memory offset within that segment. In order to come up with the 20-bit address, the value in the segment register is multiplied by 16 or 10h (its bits are shifted left by four places) and the address of the offset is added to that value. For example, suppose that the DS register contains the value 1A36h. Then the effective address of the destination operand in the second line of the example given above would be:

```
DS × 10 + 400 = 1A36 × 10h + 400 = 1AC60h.
```

Register

Register addressing mode implies that the operand to be used is in a register.

```
mov BX, AX     ; Copies value in AX to BX
mov X, AL      ; Copies value in AL to X (DS:X)
```

Indirect (or Register Indirect)

In register indirect addressing mode, the address of one operand is stored in the BX, SI, or DI register. The address is assumed to refer to an offset within the segment pointed to by DS. If needed, the segment can be overridden by qualifying the operand with another segment register.

```
mov ES:[DI], CX     ; Copy CX to the effective
                    ;   address: ES × 10h + DI.
```

The following code fragment stores CAFEh in the effective address 1AC67h when DS = 1A36h:

```
mov CX, 0CAFEh     ; Which addressing mode is this?
mov BX, 907h
mov [BX], CX       ; This is a Register Indirect MOVe.
```

Base-displacement (or Based Relative)

Base-displacement addressing mode is employed by instructions that use either of the base registers, BX or BP, in the calculation of the effective address of an operand. When BX is used, the effective address is implicitly determined by the value in DS along with any offsets supplied as part of the instruction. In the instruction,

```
mov AX, [BX]+9  ; equivalent to mov AX, [BX+9]
```

the effective address of the source operand is given by:

```
DS × 10h + BX + 9
```

When BP is involved in the instruction, the effective address is implicitly determined by the value in SS along with any offsets supplied as part of the instruction. Thus, the source operand in the instruction,

```
mov AX, [BP]+9
```

has the effective address:

```
SS × 10h + BP + 9.
```

The default segments, DS and SS, can be overridden by providing a segment register explicitly in the instruction, such as in:

```
mov AX, DS:[BP]+9
```

Base-Index (and Based-indexed with displacement)

Based indexed addressing mode is, as you might expect, a combination of based and indexed addressing mode. One register, BX or BP, holds the base address, and DI or SI supplies the index. Either one of the base registers can be combined with either one of the index registers, and a displacement can be used with any of these. The effective address of the destination operand of:

```
mov [BX][DI]+3, CX
```

is

```
DS × 16 + BX + DI + 3.
```

As with based relative and indexed addressing, the default segment, DS, can be overridden, as in:

```
mov AX, SS:[BX][SI]+14
```

Alternative Syntax

An equivalent syntax for based indexed instructions uses only one set of brackets, as in:

```
mov AX, SS:[BX+SI+14]
```

Similarly, for based displacement (relative) indexing we can write:

```
mov AX, [BX+9]
```

instead of:

```
mov AX, [BX]+9
```

As a practical matter, it is usually better to let the assembler handle the subtleties of addressing a program's variables. Just about every program that we write will contain something similar to this:

```
.DATA
Count     DB 0h
          :
          :                    ; Other data declarations
          :
          .CODE
ProgName  PROC                 ; Main part of program
          mov AX, @DATA        ; Point DS to data segment
          mov DS, AX           ;    above.
          :
          mov CL, Count        ; The assembler figures out
          :                    ;    this address for us.
```

```
ProgName    ENDP
END         ProgName
```

If the variable Count is in a segment other than DS, the segment can be overridden directly in the instruction through use of an explicit segment:

```
mov CL, ES:Count
```

Helpful Additional Data Movement Instructions

Suppose the need arises to swap the contents of two registers or the contents of memory with a register or vice versa. We could write:

```
mov AX, CX
mov CX, BX
mov BX, AX
```

to swap the values in CX and BX. Alternatively, we can use the XCHG instruction:

```
xchg BX, CX
```

One of the operands for the XCHG instruction can be a memory location:

```
xchg Count, CX
```

Using XCHG is slightly more efficient than the explicit move sequence shown in the first example mostly because no additional steps (or additional memory or registers) are required to preserve and restore the contents of the temporary register.

Many of the data movement instructions described above rely on some knowledge of the address of a memory operand. We mentioned that it is usually easier to let the assembler take care of address details. This approach may not always be appropriate. If the actual address of an operand is needed, there are two ways of obtaining the actual address of a memory operand. The first is through use of the LEA, or load the effective address, instruction.

```
lea SI, Count
```

Although BX, BP, SI, and DI, are probably the most useful, the destination of the LEA instruction can be any 16-bit register.

A slightly faster way to do the same thing is to use the keyword OFFSET. The two instructions shown below are equivalent:

```
lea SI, Count
mov SI, OFFSET Count
```

The particular one that you choose is a matter of style.

4.2   Arithmetic Operations

4.2.1 Addition

The various addressing modes just discussed apply to any operation that accepts a memory address as one of its operands. For instance, the ADD instruction can take any of the following forms:

```
add AX, 3              ; Immediate
add CX, BX             ; Register
add Sum, CX            ; Direct
add DX, [BX]           ; Register Indirect
add AL, [BP]+5         ; Base-Displacement
add [BX][SI]+4, CH     ; Base-Indexed Displacement
```

In all cases, the source operand is added to the destination operand that holds the bitwise sum. As with the MOV instruction, the source and destination operands must be the same size.

The ADD instruction affects several flags as shown in Table 4.1.

4.2.2 Subtraction

The format and addressing modes of the 80x86 subtraction instruction are identical to those of the addition instruction:

```
sub <destination>, <source>
```

Table 4.1   80x86 Arithmetic Flags

Flag Name	Is set (=1) to indicate that:
Carry flag (CF)	In an 8-bit operation, a carry out from the eighth bit (D7) has occurred in a system operation, or a carry out from the sixteenth bit (D15) has occurred in a word operation.
Overflow flag (OF)	In an 8-bit operation, the carry in and carry out are different, as found in D7, for a byte sum, DIS for a word sum.
Zero flag (ZF)	The result is zero.
Sign flag (SF)	The result is negative.
Parity flag (PF)	The result contains an odd number of bits.
Auxiliary flag (AF)	The result contains a carry out of D4. (This flag is useful in BCD arithmetic.)

80x86 subtraction is carried out by adding the two's complement of the source to the destination. If the result is negative, the sign, carry, and auxiliary flags are set to 1.

4.2.3 Increment and Decrement

The need for adding or subtracting 1 from a memory variable or register is so common that Intel has provided two instructions for this purpose: INC and DEC. The operand can be either a register or memory address.

```
inc AX    ; Add 1 to AX
inc Y     ; Add 1 to variable Y
dec BX    ; Subtract 1 from BX
dec Y     ; Subtract 1 from variable Y
```

These instructions are more concise and much more efficient than their addition and subtraction equivalents:

```
add AX, 1
add Y,  1
sub BX, 1
sub Y,  1
```

4.2.4 Multiplication and Division

80x86 assembly provides two separate multiplication and division instructions for signed and unsigned operations. MUL and DIV assume that both operands are unsigned numbers, whereas IMUL and IDIV consider the signs of both operands. For byte operations, all four of these instructions assume that one of the operands is in AX, and for word operations the combination of DX and AX is used.

For example, AX contains 110h after the following code snippet is executed:

```
mov AL, 11h
mov BL, 10h
mul BL        ; Multiplies AL by 10h
```

For word multiplication, the product is stored in DX:AX. (We indicate this 32-bit combination with the notation DX:AX.) After the following program fragment executes, DX contains 001Ah and AX contains 0B00h.

```
mov DX, 0
mov AX, 1AB0h
mov BX, 100h
mul BX        ; Multiplies AX by 100h
```

After this code fragment executes, the overflow and carry flags are both set to 1.

To see the difference between MUL and IMUL, consider the two code fragments below:

```
mov DX, 0       ; Unsigned multiplication
mov AX, -1d
mov BX, 100h
mul BX
```

```
mov DX, 0       ; Signed multiplication
mov AX, -1d
mov BX, 100h
imul BX
```

After the first fragment executes, DX:AX contains 00FF:FF00. After the second fragment executes DX:AX contains FFFF:FF00.

The behavior of the DIV and IDIV instructions is analogous to MUL and IMUL. For byte arithmetic, the dividend is placed in AX, and in DX:AX for word arithmetic. The divisor can be a register or memory operand. In byte division, the quotient is placed in AH and the remainder in AL. Word division returns the quotient in AX and the remainder in DX. Indeed, it is possible for a quotient to be too large to fit into its defined register destination. Such a situation arises when we attempt division of DX:AX = 0001:0000 by 1. The quotient will not fit into AX alone. This operation—as well as division by zero—causes an interrupt to occur within the processor and the program halts.

The example below performs unsigned byte division to determine that 14 ÷ 4 = 3 with a remainder of 2.

```
mov AX, OEh     ; AH = 0, AL = 14d
mov BX, 04h     ; BH = 0, BL = 04d
div BL          ; AH = 3, AL = 2
```

4.2.5 Assembler Arithmetic Helpers

Making sure that source operands for arithmetic operations are the proper size and sign is crucial to correct program operation. Consider the instruction:

```
mul [BX]
```

You can't tell whether the instruction involves a byte or a word, and the assembler can't either. Most assemblers will issue a warning, but will go ahead and assume that you are calling for a word operation. If this is not the case, you probably won't get the results that you expect. (And it will be very hard to find the error!) To make your intentions explicit, you should qualify instructions that involve pointers with a PTR directive. The PTR directive is also useful for overriding the defined storage type for an operand (e.g., using only one byte of a word).

```
mul BYTE PTR [BX]        ; The multiplier is a byte!
```

If your program involves arithmetic using both bytes and words, you will find that the CBW (convert-byte-to-word) instruction will come in handy. CBW converts the value in AL to a word in AX. The AX register is always assumed and the instruction takes no operands. Consider what happens when the following code fragment executes:

```
mov  AL, -1
mov  CX, 1
imul CX
```

One might think that DX:AX contains FFFFh = -1d, but this is not the case (unless AH also contained -1) because we have performed word arithmetic using byte values. If we convert the value in AL to a word before performing the multiplication, the result is what we would expect:

```
mov  AX, 0
mov  AL, -1     ; AX = 0000 FFFF
cbw             ; AX = FFFF FFFF
mov  CX, 1
imul CX
```

CBW comes in handy especially when performing signed byte division. The dividend must be a word, even if its value is provided by byte storage. Similarly, CWD converts the word in AX to a double word in DX:AX, preserving the sign of the value in AX.

4.2.6 Review Questions

1. What is the effective address of the following if DS = 57B3h?

   ```
   mov CX, OBEEFh
   mov DI, 0102A
   mov [DI], CX
   ```

2. Is the following instruction legal? Explain.

   ```
   mov BX, AH
   ```

3. Is the following instruction legal? Explain.

   ```
   mov [BX], AH
   ```

4. Is the following instruction legal? Explain.

   ```
   mov AX, [SI][DI]+3
   ```

5. Write alternative code for:

   ```
   sub AX, 1
   add BX, 1
   ```

6. When dealing with signed numbers, prior to executing a division operation it is often a good idea to execute the _____ or _____ instruction to assure the dividend contains the correct sign.

4.2.7 Programming Assignments

1. Write a program that exercises each of the arithmetic instructions described in this section. Trace your program in your favorite debugger. Which instructions cause the value of a flag to change? Which flags changed and why did they change?

4.3   Control Structures

4.3.1 Branching Statements

Unconditional Jump

The simplest branching instruction is the unconditional jump, the mnemonic for which in 80x86 assembly language is JMP. The operand of a JMP statement is an address, which can be in the same segment or in a different segment. The address of the jump is expressed as a displacement—positive or negative—from the location of the jump instruction. Thus, a jump that reduces the value in the IP register would have a negative displacement. An unqualified jump target assumes the target is between −32768 and +32767 bytes of the location of the JMP instruction. This is called a **near jump**. The format is:

```
JMP MyLabel     ; MyLabel is defined in the same segment.
JMP BX          ; Assumes BX contains a valid address.
                ; Any nonsegment register can be used.
JMP [BX]        ; The address of the jump target is
                ; at the memory address pointed to by BX.
```

When branching to an address within a displacement of −128 and +127 bytes of the current value in the IP register, using the SHORT directive produces a two byte instruction rather than a three byte instruction.

```
jmp SHORT MyLabel      ; MyLabel must be in the
                       ; same segment and within a
                       ; signed 8-bit displacement
                       ; range.
```

It is also possible to jump into another segment. This is called a **far jump** and it potentially alters the values stored in both CS and IP. A far jump label must be declared within the same segment as the JMP instruction. The assembler reserves four bytes for the address and the linker supplies the actual address. We have provided an example below.

```
          .CODE
          :
MyLabel   LABEL FAR
          :
MyProc    PROC
          :

          :
          jmp FAR PTR MyLabel
          :

          :
MyProc    ENDP
          :
```

Conditional Jump

Every high level language includes a conditional statement that resembles:

```
IF Oper1 <logical operator> Oper2 THEN
     [Imperative statement(s)]
ELSE
     [Imperative statement(s)]
ENDIF
```

The syntax varies from one language to another, but the idea is the same. Based on the outcome of the comparison, program execution proceeds along one path or another.

In 80x86 assembly language, the IF part of the comparison is replaced by CMP:

```
CMP <destination>, <source>
```

The operands can be two registers, or a register and a memory location, as explained in the previous Data Movement section. The result of the comparison sets flags OF, SF, ZF, AF, PF, and CF. The state of these flags is the same as if <source> had been subtracted from <destination>, because this is indeed what happens in the accumulator. The instruction following the comparison is usually a signed or an unsigned conditional jump that branches to the specified label based on the state of the flags as shown in Table 4.2.

We observe that the mnemonics for unsigned jumps are described by "above" and "below," while the signed jumps are described by "greater than" or "less than." To make matters more confusing, many of the

Table 4.2 Conditional Branching Instructions

Unsigned Mnemonic	Signed Mnemonic	Jump Executed when Flag(s)	Meaning
JE JZ	JE JE	ZF = 1	Jump if equal.
JNE JNZ	JNE JNZ	ZF = 0	Jump if not equal.
JA JNBE		CF = 0 or ZF = 0	Jump when source above (greater than) (or not below/less than) or equal to destination.
	JG JNLE	SF = OF or ZF = 0	
JB JNAE		CF = 1	Jump when source below (less than) (or not above greater than or equal to) destination.
	JL JNGE	SF ≠ OF	
JAE JNB		CF = 0	Jump when source above (greater than) (or not below/less than) or equal to destination.
	JGE JNL	SF = OF	
JBE JNA		CF = 1 or ZF = 1	Jump when source below (less than) (or not above/greater than) or equal to destination.
	JLE JNG	ZF = 1 and SF ≠ OF	

mnemonics support equivalent negated forms. For example, asking whether something is greater than something else is equivalent to asking whether it is not less than and not equal to something else.

While these instructions are most useful following a CMP, it is interesting to note that the comparison instruction is not required. The only thing that the conditional branching instructions really do is interrogate the status of certain flags. How they get set is completely at the discretion of the programmer. (See the programming assignment at the end of Section 4.4.4 for an unconventional approach.)

4.3.2 Iteration

Arithmetic and comparison instructions enable us to write code blocks that repeat for a given number of iterations. In a higher-level language, we often write something resembling:

```
FOR A = 1 TO 10 DO
        :
        [Group of statements]
        :

ENDDO
```

Translating this directly to assembly language, we could write:

```
        mov CX, 10
Start:  :
        [Group of statements]
        :
        dec CX
        jnz SHORT Start  ; Falls through to Done when CX = 0
Done:   :
        [More statements]
        :
```

This sort of code is so common that Intel provides a shorthand way of doing exactly the same thing with the LOOP instruction. To use LOOP, place the number of desired iterations into CX, and the processor takes care of the rest, as follows:

```
        mov CX, 10
Start:      :
        [Group of statements]
        :
        loop Start     ; Falls through to Done when CX = 0
Done:   :
        [More statements]
        :
```

This approach works fine until CX is needed for something else (in the body of the loop, perhaps) or the need arises to create a nested loop. In this case, we need to use other registers or (shudder!) memory and write the loop code the long way. Nevertheless, we can still save a few cycles and a few bytes by using one of the other LOOPx instructions: LOOPE, LOOPZ, LOOPNE, or LOOPNZ. Each of these instructions automatically decrements CX, just like the LOOP instruction, but the comparison also takes into account the zero flag.

LOOPNE and LOOPNZ jump to the loop label only while CX and the zero flag are both nonzero. If either are zero, execution falls to the next statement. The following code fragment demonstrates a nested loop with the outer loop being executed twice and the inner loop three times.

```
        mov AX, 2              ; Initialize outer loop variable.
Outer:  [Group of "outer" statements.]
        mov CX, 3              ; Initialize inner loop variable.
Inner:  [Group of "inner" statements.]
        loop Inner
        dec AX
        loopnz Outer
```

LOOPE and LOOPZ work in a similar manner, except that the jump is executed when CX is nonzero and the zero flag is 1. Of course, with both sets of LOOPx instructions, you need to be mindful of the value in CX. If CX = 1 *before* the LOOPx instruction is executed, the loop will terminate regardless of the value of the zero flag.

4.3.3 Review Questions

1. The following code fragment is supposed to execute until AX = 0. Suppose CX = 1 when the DEC AX instruction is executed. What happens? How do you fix it?

```
        mov AX, 2
        :
Top:    [Group of statements.]
        :
        dec AX
        loopnz Top
```

2. Assuming that the instructions inside the brackets ([...]) are the same, will the two code fragments that follow produce identical results? Explain.

```
; --- Fragment #1 ---
          mov AX, 2     ; Initialize outer loop variable.
Outer:    [Group of "outer" statements]
          mov BX, 3     ; Initialize inner loop variable.
Inner:    dec BX
          [Group of "inner" statements]
          loopnz Inner
          dec AX
          loopnz Outer


; --- Fragment #2 ---
          mov AX, 2     ; Initialize outer loop variable.
Outer:    [Group of "outer" statements]
          mov CX, 3     ; Initialize inner loop variable.
Inner:    [Group of "inner" statements]
          loop Inner
          dec AX
          loopnz Outer
```

3. For each of the following below, determine if the jump is executed, given:

   ▪ the contents of "AX" and "value"
   ▪ the instruction immediately preceding the jump instruction, and
   ▪ the jump instruction.

AX	Value	Instruction Before Jump	Jump Instruction	(Circle correct answer) Jump to Destination?
a) 004F	FF38	cmp AX, value	jl dest	YES or NO
b) 004F	FF38	cmp AX, value	jb dest	YES or NO
c) 004F	004F	cmp AX, value	je dest	YES or NO
d) 004F	0079	cmp AX, value	jne dest	YES or NO
e) —	FF38	cmp value, 0	jbe dest	YES or NO
f) —	FF38	cmp value, -200	jge dest	YES or NO
g) 004F	—	add AX, 200	js dest	YES or NO
h) —	FF38	add value, 200	jz dest	YES or NO

4. Rewrite each of the following program segments in assembly language code:

a)
```
if (ax > 0) and (total < 10) then
    ax = ax + total
    total = total + 1
else
    ax = ax + 1
    total = total – ax
endif
```

b
```
while (value > 100) or (count < 50) do
    value = value – 5
    count = count + 1
endwhile
```

4.3.4 Programming Assignments

1. Write a triple nested loop that adds 1 to AX on the innermost iteration of the loop. Construct the loop so that the innermost statement executes 4 times, the middle loop executes 3 times, and the outermost loop runs twice.

2. Write a program to calculate the Fibonacci series: 1,1,2,3,4,8,13, [...] Given the first two terms, each successive term is the sum of the preceding terms. Use the LOOP instruction and iterate 12 times. Place the last term in the AX register.

4.4   Boolean and Other Bit Manipulation Instructions

4.4.1 Boolean Operations

We usually program in assembly language for one of two reasons: to squeeze as much work as possible from each machine cycle, or to interact with the machine at a level that is impossible with higher level languages. When we use assembly language, we can manipulate the value of any bit that is visible to the program. The basic Boolean operations, AND, OR, NOT, and XOR, provide the means by which we may examine and manipulate individual bits in registers or memory. The formats of these instructions are:

```
AND <destination>, <source>
OR  <destination>, <source>
XOR <destination>, <source>
NOT <destination>
```

where the destination can be a register or memory, and the source can be an immediate value, a register, or memory (unless the destination is also memory).

The AND operation is especially useful for masking off certain bits. For example, suppose we are interested in only the lower 2 bits of AH and the upper 2 bits of AL. All other bits will be set to zero with:

```
and AX, 03C0h
```

AND, OR, and XOR always set the carry and overflow flags to zero. (Why?) The parity, zero, and sign flags are set according to the outcome of the operation. Thus, a quick way to check whether a register or memory is zero is:

```
AND <destination>, <destination>
```

For example, the code segment:

```
and AX, AX
jz <aLabel>
```

tests whether AX is zero without changing the value in AX. The program path will jump to the indicated label if AX is zero.

XOR comes in handy for efficiently zeroing out a register. The instruction,

```
xor BX, BX
```

sets the BX register to zero.

The NOT operation gives us the one's complement, or (equivalently) the logical complement of the operand. No flags are affected by this operation. The logical NOT is not to be confused with the NEG operation, which gives the two's complement and sets the auxiliary, carry, overflow, parity, sign, and zero flags in accordance with the outcome of the operation.

4.4.2 Bit Shifting Operations

Another way in which we can manipulate individual bits in the 80x86 is through **shifting,** or moving the value stored in a register or in memory to the left or right by one or more bit positions. The 80x86 provides two types of shift instructions: **logical shifts** and **arithmetic shifts**.

Logical Bit Shifting

The carry flag participates in a logical shift operation by storing the last bit shifted out of the operand. The operand's leftmost or rightmost vacated bits with zeroes. For example, suppose AX stores F00Bh. The bit pattern is: 1111 0000 0000 1011. The value in AX is shifted to the right by one bit after executing:

```
shr AX, 1
```

AX now contains 0111 1000 0000 0101 (or 7805h) and the carry flag is set to 1. We observe that the most significant bit has been filled with zero.

If we want to shift right by two or more bits, the assembler will complain if we write, for example:

```
shr AX, 3              ; Can't do this!
```

In order to carry out a multiple bit shift, place the number of positions to rotate into CL, then give CL as an operand, as in the instruction:

```
mov CL, 3              ; Note: CL MUST be used!
shr AX, CL
```

The logical left shift works the same way as the right shift, only in the other direction. If BX contains B00Fh = 1011 0000 0000 1111 and we execute:

```
shl BX, 1
```

BX will contain 0110 0000 0001 1110 and the carry flag will be 1.

In the SHR and SHL instructions, we may lose the values stored in the bits that are shifted out of the operand because once the bit exits the carry flag, we have no way to get it back. Sometimes we need to retain all bit values through a right or left shift operation. The **rotate instructions** do this for us.

In the rotate right instruction, ROR, each bit is shifted one position to the right except for the rightmost bit, which ends up in the carry flag and also in the high-order bit of the operand.

Consider the following code fragment:

```
        mov  CX, 10h
        mov  AX, 1
Next:   ror  AX, 1
        loop Next
```

Initially, AX is 0001h. The first pass through the loop, AX becomes 8000h, and the carry flag is set to 1. The overflow flag is also set to 1 because the two high-order bits in AX differ from each other. After the second pass through the loop, AX = 4000h, CF = 0, and OV = 1. (Why?) By tracing this code in your favorite debugger, you can actually watch the bit rotate through all 16 positions in AX.

You can observe the reverse action that ROL provides by tracing the following program fragment:

```
        mov  CX, 10h
        mov  AX, 1
Next:   rol  AX, 1
        loop Next
```

As with the logical shift instructions, the CL register specifies the number of bits to shift in the execution of a single instruction.

It may seem odd to you that the carry bit always contains a copy of one of the bits in the operand. The flag gives us an extra bit; why can't we use it for something? We can indeed, by using the RCL and RCR instructions. They treat the carry flag as if it were a ninth bit. The usage of RCL and RCR is the same as discussed previously with ROL and ROR.

Arithmetic Bit-Shifting
Arithmetic bit shifting differs from logical bit shifting and may seem confusing at first. The arithmetic shift left instruction, SAL, has exactly the same binary code as SHL, and produces the same behavior in the microprocessor. Thus, if we have −32767 (8001h) in the operand, say AX, and then we execute:

```
sal AX, 1
```

AX becomes 0002h (with flags OF = CF = 1). We might have expected the high-order bit to remain 1 so that the sign is preserved. However, the sign bit is retained in the arithmetic shift right instruction, SAR. Thus, if AX = 8001h, the instruction:

```
sar AX, 1
```

produces AX = 1100 0000 0000 0000 = C000h. If we execute the instruction again, AX will be E000h.

We note that there are some similarities between arithmetic shifting and multiplication and division by 2. When all operands are positive and less than or equal to 7FFFh, the operations are equivalent. So when small operands are involved, bit shifting offers a much faster alternative to multiplication or division by 2.

4.4.3 Review Questions

1. We said that ANDing a register with itself sets the zero flag, if the register contains all zeroes. Would OR do the same thing?

2. Suppose that we need to make sure that the two high-order bits of both AH and AL are always 1. Write a single instruction to do this.

3. Suppose that we need to make sure that the two high-order bits of both AH and AL are never 1. Write a single instruction to do this.

4. If the beginning value stored in AX = 3, what value is stored in AX after the following code fragment executes?

   ```
   not AX
   mov BX, AX
   neg AX
   add AX, BX
   ```

5. If the beginning value stored in AX = 3, what value is stored in AX after the following code fragment executes?

   ```
   neg AX
   mov BX, AX
   not AX
   add AX, BX
   ```

6. Is the following code fragment legal? Explain.

   ```
   mov CL, 17d
   shr AX, CL
   ```

7. Under what conditions will the overflow flag be set (1) when the SAR instruction is executed?

8. What are the contents of the specified registers at the points indicated in the following code?

   ```
   A       DB      0Ah, 1Ah, 2Ah, 3Ah, 4Ah, 5Ah
   B       DW      0Bh, 1Bh, 2Bh, 3Bh, 4Bh
   ```

   ```
   mov   AL, [A]  ;         AL = _____
   mov   AL, [A+3] ;        AL = _____
   mov   AX, [B+2] ;        AX = _____
   mov   AX, [B+6] ;        AX = _____
   mov   AX, [B-2] ;        AX = _____
   ```

```
mov   AL, 11001010b
shr   AL, 1 ;          AL = _____
mov   AL, 11001010b
sar   AL, 1 ;          AL = _____
mov   AL, 11001010b
ror   AL, 1 ;          AL = _____
mov   AL, 11001010b
shl   AL, 1 ;          AL = _____
mov   AL, 11001010b
sal   AL, 1 ;          AL = _____
mov   AL, 11001010b
rol   AL, 1 ;          AL = _____
mov   CL, 5
mov   AL, 11001010b
rol   AL, CL ;         AL = _____
mov   AL, 0Fh
shl   AL, 1 ;          AL = _____
mov   AL, 11001010b
and   AL, 01111000b ;  AL = _____
mov   AL, 11001010b
or    AL, 01111000b ;  AL = _____
mov   AL, 11001010b
xor   AL, 01111000b ;  AL = _____
```

9. Write a code fragment that preserves the sign of the operand when a SAL instruction is executed.

4.4.4 Programming Assignments

1. Write a program to perform division and multiplication by 2 on integer values using the shift operator. Since we don't know how to output integer values yet, leave the result in the AX register.

2. As you know, flags are just binary values stored in a flags register. Some of these flags can be manipulated like any binary value stored in a register. There are two complementary instructions for this purpose: the load-flags-to-AH instruction, LAHF, and the save-flags-from-AH instruction, SAHF. Neither of these instructions takes an operand. The flags are stored to, and loaded from, these bit positions:

Bits of AH (high-order to low-order)							
D7	D6	D5	D4	D3	D2	D1	D0
SF	ZF		AF		PF		CF

While they are in AH, they can be ANDed, ORed, XORed, and shifted to produce whatever behavior we like. Use these facts in a program that exercises all of the jump instructions discussed in the previous section.

Chapter 5

Arrays and Strings

5.1 Arrays

At the assembly language level, strings and arrays are the two principal data structures that make it easy for us to access and manipulate values stored in contiguous memory space. The mnemonics for array declaration are straightforward: all you need to do is reserve some space in your program. You are not even required to give this space a name, although that will make your life easier. The general format for an array declaration looks like any other declaration except that we augment the definition with the number of elements to set aside and, optionally, any initializations.

Some examples of 80x86 array declarations are:

```
BArray1 DB 10 DUP(0)       ; Allocates 10 bytes of memory
                           ;   at address referenced by
                           ;   BArray1. The 10 bytes will
                           ;   be initialized with 0s.

BArray2 DB 10 DUP(?)       ; Allocates 10 bytes of memory
                           ;   at address referenced by
                           ;   BArray2. The 10 bytes will
                           ;   not be initialized.

BArray3 DB '0','1','2','3','4'   ; Allocates 10 bytes and
        DB '5','6','7','8','9'   ;   initializes them with
                                 ;     numeric characters.
```

```
WArray1 DW 10 DUP(0ABBAh) ; Allocates 10 words of memory
                          ;    at address referenced by
                          ;    WArray1. The 10 words will
                          ;    be initialized with ABBAs.
```

We can make BArray3 look just like BArray1 by filling BArray2 with zeroes. To do this, we construct a loop and employ based relative addressing to access each array element:

```
       mov SI, 10d             ; Load array size into SI.
Next:  dec SI                  ; Use SI for the offset from
       mov [BArray3+SI], 0     ;   the address of BArray3.
       jnz SHORT Next          ; When SI is zero, we're
                               ;   done. (Flag set in DEC
                               ;   instruction.)
```

Doing the same thing to WArray1 is a bit trickier because we are dealing with words, not bytes. This means that the address of each element increases by 2 as we iterate through the array:

```
       mov CX, 10              ; Load element count into CX.
Next:  mov SI, CX              ; Move count into index reg.
       dec SI                  ; Decrement for indexing.
       shl SI, 1               ; Multiply offset by 2
       mov [WArray1+SI], 0     ;   because array element
       loop Next               ;   size is 2.
```

As explained in Appendix A of your text, arrays consist of linear memory that is accessed in logical blocks (e.g., rows and columns) by a program. Thus, the C declarations:

```
char arrayA1[6];
char arrayA2[2][3];
char arrayA3[3][2];
```

reserve identical amounts of storage at run time.

We can do the same in an 80x86 assembly language program using a similar syntax:

```
arrayA1 DB 6 DUP(?)
arrayA2 DB 2 DUP(3 DUP(?))
arrayA3 DB 3 DUP(2 DUP(?))
```

Unlike Java, or any other higher-level language, assembly language gives us no concise way to access the array by rows and columns. We have to manage that for ourselves. Consequently, we have a choice whether to access the array in row major or column major mode.

For example, if we have a two-dimensional array consisting of 4 rows and 3 columns of bytes, one method to access each element in the third row of the array is as follows:

```
; Store the integers 6, 7, and 8 into
;   the first second and third elements of the
;   third row of a 4 x 3 array.

arrayA4     DB    4 DUP(3 DUP(?))
numRows     DB    4                    ; There are four rows.
rowLength   DB    3                    ; There are three columns.

      mov BX, 0
      mov AL, rowLength
      mov BL, 2                    ; We want the third row.
      mul BL                       ; AX now contains the offset
                                   ;   to the first element of
                                   ;   the third row of the
                                   ;   array.
      mov SI, AX                   ; Use SI + BX as an index
      mov BX, 0                    ;   with SI storing the row
                                   ;   and BX the column.

      mov DX, 6                    ; A value to put in the array.
Top:  mov [arrayA4+SI+BX], DL      ; Store the value.
      inc DL
      inc BL                       ; Point to next element.
      cmp rowLength, BL
      loopnz Top
```

This idea can be extended to any number of dimensions by keeping in mind the size of the offsets needed to get to any particular element of the array.

5.2　Strings

In higher-level languages we think of a string as a group of characters stored contiguously, as in the following C declaration:

```
char data[10] = "0123456789";
```

An equivalent string declaration in 80x86 assembly language is:

```
data DB '0123456789'
```

and so is:

```
data DB     48,49,50,51,52,53,54,55,56,57
```

and so is:

```
data DW     3130h, 3332h, 3534h, 3736h, 3938h
```

80x86 strings are actually one-dimensional arrays. Their data type is always a series of contiguous binary values. The 80x86 supports a number of instructions to make string movement and comparison relatively easy. The general idea in using all of them is that you:

1. Tell the program how long the string is (by placing a value in CX).
2. Tell the program where to find the strings.
3. Set the direction flag.
4. Repeat the instruction over the length of the string.

The "move byte string" instruction (MOVSB), which copies a byte string from one location to another, nicely illustrates 80x86 string handling.

Suppose a program contains the following declarations:

```
Data1    DB   1,2,3,4,5,6,7,8
Data2    DB   8 DUP (?)
```

and that Data1 needs to be copied to Data2 at some point. The MOVSB instruction expects the source string (Data1 in this case) to be pointed to by DS:SI and the destination string (Data2) to be pointed to by ES:DI. As a result, we need to load these registers with suitable pointers. If the program occupies only one segment, its code segments and data segments are the same. At runtime, CS contains the required value, and DS and ES will probably hold the same value. If you want to be certain, the value of CS can be copied to DS and ES:

```
mov AX, CS    ; Do this when the program
mov DS, AX    ;   occupies only one segment.
mov ES, AX
```

In a multi-segment program, you would do the following: Establish correct values in DS and ES:

```
mov AX, @DATA    ; Do this when the program
mov DS, AX       ;   occupies multiple segments.
mov ES, AX
```

Point SI and DI to the correct locations and clear the direction flag:

```
mov SI, offset Data1
mov DI, offset Data2
cld
```

Place the length of the string in CX and repeat the move instruction, decrementing CX until CX is zero.

```
mov CX, 08
rep MOVSB
```

The effect of the above example is equivalent to the following:

```
        mov CX, 8
        mov BX, 0

Top:    mov AL, BYTE PTR [Data1+BX]
        mov BYTE PTR [Data2+BX], AL
        inc BX
        loop Top
```

This code performs a byte-by-byte copy of Data1 to Data2. The index into each starts at zero and increases to the size of the strings. This behavior is controlled by the status of the direction flag, which we set to zero using the CLD instruction. In this case, we could have just as easily started at the high end of the strings and worked back to zero by setting the direction flag with the STD instruction.

All of the 80x86 string operations have both a byte form and a word form. If Data1 and Data2 were strings of words instead of bytes, the MOVSW instruction would be used instead:

```
Data1   DW   1,2,3,4,5,6,7,8
Data2   DW   8 DUP (?)
        :
        [All other instructions are the same]
        :
        mov CX, 08
        rep MOVSW
```

Other handy shortcuts include the store-to-string instructions, STOSB and STOSW. These instructions take the current value of AL or AX and place it into the string location specified. If this instruction is repeated over the length of the string, the entire string is initialized to the value in AX. The sequence typically reads as follows:

```
AString    DW    8 DUP (?)

    mov AX, CS                  ; Assume AString is in the
    mov ES, AX                  ;    code segment.

    mov DI, offset AString

    xor AX, AX                  ; Zero out AX
    mov CX, 08
    rep STOSB                   ; Move all zeroes into AString
```

The inverse of the STOSB instruction is the LODSB. LODSB loads AX with the values contained in the string pointed to by DS:SI. Although you can specify a repetition by loading CX with a value and using the REP prefix, there isn't much point in doing so. AX will always contain only the last value loaded from the string.

To search a string for a particular value, the 80x86 provides the "scan string" instruction SCASB for byte strings and SCASW for word strings. One of the prefixes REPE (REPZ) or REPNE (REPNZ) is typically used in conjunction with a scan string. The comparison value is stored in AL if the string consists of bytes and AX if the string consists of words. REPNE causes the scan to continue until a match is found; REPE causes the scan to continue while the values in the string match the value in AX. As usual, CX contains the length of the string, and the string's location is in ES:DI.

Suppose we want to see whether a string called Data1 contains the ASCII escape character. The following program fragment illustrates how we could do this using SCASB:

```
Data1 DB        8 DUP (?)

    mov AX, DS                  ; Assume Data1 is in the
    mov ES, AX                  ;    data segment.

    mov DI, offset Data1
    cld                         ; Search up starting from the
                                ;    start of Data1 (low address).
    mov AL, 01Bh                ; ASCII escape character.
    mov CX, 08                  ; String length.
    repnz                       ; Scan the string until we find
    scasb                       ;    a match or CX = 0.
    jz FoundIt                  ; If the zero flag is set,
                                ;    we have a match!

    [Processing for no match found]

    jmp Done
FoundIt:
```

```
          [Processing for a match]
Done:   . . .
```

The preceding code is equivalent to this code:

```
Data1 DB   8 DUP (?)

          mov AL, 01Bh       ; ASCII escape character
          mov CX, 08         ; String length
          xor BX, BX

Top:      cmp AL, BYTE PTR [Data1+BX]
          jz FoundIt
          inc BX
          loop Top

          [Processing for no match found]

      jmp Done
FoundIt:
          [Processing for a match]
Done:     . . .
```

Individual bytes or words are located in strings using SCASB or SCASW, respectively. While it is possible to use these instructions to see whether two entire strings match, it would be tedious to do so. It is easier (and briefer) to use the CMPSB and CMPSW instructions for this purpose. These instructions are used in a manner consistent with the operation of the MOVSB instruction, with the source operand in the DS:SI address, and the destination in the ES:DI address. CX contains the number of characters to compare, and, as before, the direction flag indicates whether the strings are compared up from their low addresses or down from their high addresses. When the REPE (or REPZ) prefix is used in conjunction with a string comparison instruction, the comparison stops when the first value that differs is found. If the strings are identical, the zero flag will be set following the last execution of CMPSB or CMPSW. For example:

```
String1  DB  1,2,3,4,5,6,7,8
String2  DB  8 DUP (?)
:
[Processing that involves String2.]
:
      mov AX, CS         ; Strings are in the same
      mov DS, AX         ;   segment as the code.
      mov ES, AX
      cld
```

```
        mov SI, offset String1
        mov DI, offset String2
        mov CX, 08
        repe CMPSB
        jz  StrMatch        ; If the zero flag is set,
                            ;   we have a match.
                :
                [Steps taken when the strings differ]
                :
                jmp Done
                :
StrMatch:       [Steps taken when the strings are identical]
                :
Done:           [Next steps after string comparison]
                :
```

5.3 Bug Resistant String and Array Handling

It is tempting to make assumptions about the state of the processor when beginning a code block that executes string instructions. Specifically, if you specify a small or tiny model in the source code, DS and ES should always point to CS when the program is invoked. If you are writing software that will be deployed in the enterprise or as a commercial product, enhancements to the program could cause unanticipated changes to segment registers, resulting in unexpected program behavior. The same advice holds for the state of the direction flag, which is clear by default.

Good defensive programming assures that the iterator values are always appropriate to the size of the referenced string or array. For example, if a program contains an array (or string) called DaysOfWeek, it is a fairly safe bet that this array will always be at most seven positions long. However, if the size of an array or string is arbitrary or business dependent, its size can change over the useful life of the program. If a single occurrence of an iterator value is not changed when an array size changes, the program will not always perform as expected. To facilitate maintenance, an EQU directive should be used to supply the sizes of arrays, strings, and the iterators that access them. For example:

```
ARRAYSIZE EQU 31h
:
TotalSalesByPerson DB ARRAYSIZE DUP (0)
```

```
      :
mov CX, ARRAYSIZE
      :
```

The assembler converts the last two statements to:

```
TotalSalesByPerson DB 31h DUP (0)
```

and

```
mov CX, 31h
```

No matter what language you use, supplying helpful comments in the source code is the best way to improve maintainability and reliability. In the case of assembly language, verbose comments are crucial during coding and maintenance. They are critical when you are writing your code, because you can quickly compare what the code is doing with what the comments claim that the code is doing. Then, years later, when you go back to enhance your program, you will spare yourself many hours of frustration because the comments will reveal all you need to know.

5.4   Review Questions

1. Explain how the following declarations differ from each other:

   ```
   a. BArray1   DB 0,1,2,3,4
                DB 5,6,7,8,9
   b. BArray1   DB 0,1,2,3,4, _
                5,6,7,8,9
   c. BArray1   DB 10 DUP (0)
   d. BArray1   DB 10 DUP (0,1,2,3,4,5,6,7,8,9)
   ```

2. Explain what happens when the following code executes:

   ```
   String1   DW   1,2,3,4,5,6,7,8
   String2   DW   8 DUP (?)

   mov AX, CS     ; Strings are in the same
   mov DS, AX     ;   segment as the code.
   mov ES, AX

   cld

   mov SI, offset String1
   ```

```
mov DI, offset String2
mov CX, 08
rep MOVSB
```

5.5   Programming Assignments

1. Use the SCASB instruction to check whether an 8-character string contains something other than zeroes.
2. Use SCASB (instead of CMPSB) to determine whether two strings are identical.
3. Write a program that scans an array of words and locates the maximum value in that array. Since we do not yet know how to output numeric values, place the maximum value in AX.

Chapter 6

Procedures and Stacks

The 80x86 programs we have seen thus far have consisted of one "main" procedure. Intel assembly programs may contain any number of procedures, each enclosed in a PROC/ENDP statement pair identified with a unique name. Good programmers use modules when writing programs, as it provides an easy way to encapsulate functionality. Although programs can contain multiple procedures, they may not overlap each other. Multiple procedures can be in the same source file as the main code, or they can be in different files. In this supplement, we consider only those that are in the same source code file.

Although the PROC directive is used to define procedures, many assembly language programmers refer to these code segments using the more generic term **subprogram**. High-level languages typically have two types of subprograms: procedures and functions. These differ only in how they are used.

Generally, **functions** are used in evaluating expressions and return a value to the calling code (where this return value is substituted for the actual function call). For example, if we have the statement X = SQRT(N), then the square root function is called and sent the value of N; the return value is then substituted for the function call, and X is assigned that return value.

Procedures perform specific tasks, but by themselves do not return values (although parameters can be used to return values to the calling code). One would never "assign" the value of a procedure call to a variable. Instead, the procedure is executed as a mini-set of instructions that performs a task.

Assembly language subprograms can be treated as procedures or functions, depending on how they are used. However, these subprograms always have a return value (which is typically stored in the AX register); therefore, they more closely resemble C functions. If we want a C function to act like a procedure, we use the keyword VOID. In much the same way, we simply ignore the return value for an assembly language subprogram call.

6.1 Calling Procedures

To invoke a procedure, we use the CALL instruction, followed by the procedure name. The RET instruction indicates the end of the procedure and forces control to return to the instruction following the procedure call.

The CALL instruction pushes the current code location onto the stack (to store the return address) and performs an unconditional jump to the code location specified by the label (procedure name). It works very much like a simple jump, except it saves the return location, which is used by the RET instruction. The RET instruction pops a code location off the stack and then performs an unconditional jump to this location.

The basic syntax for a procedure (that is not the main procedure) is:

```
Name    PROC
        ; code for procedure
        RET
Name    ENDP
```

where Name is the user defined procedure name.

The following modification of our "Hello world" program is an example of how to use a procedure to perform the output:

```
;; This is my second program and will print
;;   Hello world using procedures
        .MODEL SMALL
        .STACK 100h
        .DATA
Message   DB      'Hello world', 13, 10, '$'
        .CODE
First   PROC
        mov     AX, @data
        mov     DS, AX
        call    PrtMsg
        mov     AL, 0
        mov     AH, 4ch     ; Return control to operating system
```

```
            int     21h
First       ENDP

PrtMsg      PROC
            mov     DX, offset Message
            mov     AH, 9h      ; 9h is the code used to 'display
                                ;   string'
            int     21h         ; Standard call for I/O
            RET
PrtMsg      ENDP

            END     First       ; Indicates end of program
```

The final END statement (END First) tells the assembler which PROC is the main procedure. Therefore the order of the procedures does not matter. Note that the PrtMsg procedure does not need to initialize DS, as does the First procedure. Although data needed in a procedure can be placed in the main data section, it creates a more readable program to associate the data with the subprogram itself. This is done by reentering the data section:

```
            ...
First       ENDP
            .DATA
            ...
            {place data for procedure here}
            ...
            .CODE
PrtMsg      PROC
            mov     DX, offset Message
            mov     AH, 9h      ; 9h is the code used to 'display
                                ;   string'
            int     21h         ; Standard call for I/O
            RET
```

If you use any labels inside the procedure, those labels are local to the procedure and cannot be recognized globally (unless explicitly made public by the programmer, which we do not cover in this supplement).

Before executing the instructions in a subprogram, it is a good idea to save registers. Certain registers will be affected by the instructions that execute within the procedure. Therefore, you must explicitly save those values before executing the subprogram and restore them before returning from the call. Typically, register values are stored on the stack by performing the following code:

```
ProcTest    PROC          ; Assume procedure will change AX, BX,
                          ;    and CX
            push   AX     ; Save the registers first
            push   BX
            push   CX
            pushf         ; Push the flag register values too!
            ...
            {procedure code here}
            ...
            popf
            pop    CX     ; Always pop in reverse order
            pop    BX
            pop    AX
            RET
ProcTest    ENDP
```

We pop in reverse order to restore the correct values to the registers. This works only if the stack is exactly the same when we execute the POP instructions as it was immediately *after* we executed the PUSH instructions. Therefore, if the subprogram uses the stack in *any* way, care must be taken to restore the stack correctly. The subprogram must pop all items that it has pushed, and *only* those items it has pushed. If this is not done, serious problems can arise. As a simple example, consider the RET instruction, which pops the top value from the stack to use as the return address (the value is pushed onto the stack by the CALL instruction). If the subroutine accidentally leaves a value on the stack, this value will be used as the return address, and the program will crash at best, and execute incorrectly in the worst case.

6.2 Passing Parameters

Procedures tend to be more useful if they can be passed parameters. **Parameters** are values that are passed to and from procedures. For example, if we write a subprogram to square a number, we can pass it the number to be squared. Subprograms can have any number of parameters; the number is limited by the method used. Passing parameters can be done in several ways: registers, memory, and the stack. The easiest way is to use registers.

Passing parameters in registers is easy to do and very fast. Before calling the procedure, you simply move the parameters into the appropriate registers. You are limited by the number of registers as to how many parameters you can pass.

Passing parameters through memory removes this limitation. It is easy to do but it can make your program larger and slower. Before calling the procedure, you need to copy the parameter values to the appropriate memory locations. This method is very similar to using registers (you use a variable in the same manner in which you use a register), but instructions that operate on registers execute more quickly.

Passing parameters using the stack is the most powerful and most versatile (flexible) method of passing parameters. The disadvantage is that it can be more complicated, particularly to the beginning programmer. To use the stack, you must first push the parameters onto the stack. For example, if we have two parameters for our procedure, we would push two words onto the stack. When we call a near procedure (the only type of procedure call we address in this supplement), the CALL statement pushes the contents of the IP onto the stack. You *must* remember this when you write the procedure code and are ready to get the parameters. If you accidentally pop this word off the stack, you can lose the return address. When you call a far procedure, the IP and then the CS are pushed onto the stack, thus requiring two words. In both cases, we need to make sure we don't accidentally remove these values. We could pop the values off the stack and save them somewhere. Then we could push them back onto the stack right before we execute a return. However, an easier method is to use the BP register. This register acts as a pointer into the stack. BP is an index register; therefore, we can access various values on the stack without pushing and popping. We use positive displacements from BP for parameters and negative displacements for local variables (local to the procedure). If we know how the stack is structured and what values are stored on the stack, we can move this pointer around to access our parameters without destroying the IP or CS values (or anything else) on the stack.

If the subprogram intends to use BP, then the value of that register should be saved before the subprogram code executes. Typically, the caller pushes the parameter values onto the stack and then executes the CALL instruction. The callee is responsible for saving registers, and, in particular, for saving and resetting BP. The following code saves and resets the value of BP:

```
MyProc   PROC
         push  BP        ; Save the BP register
         mov   BP, SP    ; Reset BP to point to SP
         ...
```

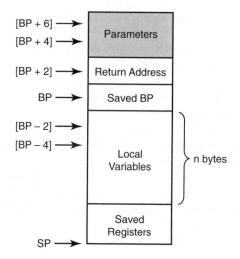

[BP + 6] ⟶   Parameters
[BP + 4] ⟶

[BP + 2] ⟶   Return Address

BP ⟶   Saved BP

[BP – 2] ⟶
[BP – 4] ⟶   Local Variables   ⎫ n bytes

   Saved Registers

SP ⟶

Figure 6.1   Stack Structure

If the subprogram needs to allocate space for local variables, this is done as follows:

```
...           ; Following the code above
sub   SP, n   ; Allocate n bytes for local variables
              ;    where n is even
```

With the previous two code segments, BP currently points to the old BP. The return address is stored at [BP+2]. The parameters are accessed using [BP+4], [BP+6], etc., assuming the CALL statement pushes *only* the IP register onto the stack (assuming a near call). The local variables are accessed by using [BP-2], [BP-4], etc. We have the stack frame as indicated in Figure 6.1.

We put all of this together in the following example. Suppose the caller wishes to call MyProc, which requires two parameters that are both words. The procedure follows:

```
MyProc    PROC
          push  BP        ; Save the BP register
          mov   BP, SP    ; Reset BP to point to SP
          sub   SP, 4     ; Allocate 4 bytes for local
                          ;    variables
          push  CX        ; Procedure uses CX register only
          ...
          {procedure code here}
          ...
```

```
        pop    CX
        mov    SP, BP     ; Deallocate local variable space
        pop    BP         ; Restore old value of BP
        RET
ProcTest ENDP
```

The program that calls MyProc is responsible for pushing the parameters onto the stack:

```
push   X        ; Put parameter X on stack
push   Y        ; Put parameter Y on stack
call   MyProc   ; Call procedure
add    SP, 4    ; Pop parameters
```

Note that instead of popping the parameters into known variables after the call returns, we simply added 4 to SP to effectively "remove" the items from the stack. It is important after a procedure call returns that the stack be restored to the exact same state it was in before the procedure was called.

The rules for using subprograms with parameters passed on the stack are summarized as follows:

1. The calling code should push the parameters onto the stack. It is helpful if they are pushed in reverse order (last parameter first). Since the stack grows downward, this stores the first parameter at the lowest address.
2. The CALL instruction places the return address on top of the parameters on the stack.
3. The subprogram should immediately push the value of BP onto the stack and copy the value of SP into BP.
4. Space for local variables can then be allocated on the stack. Since the stack grows down, the stack pointer should be decremented to do this. The amount depends on the number of local variables the subprogram needs, and this is achieved by subtracting an even number from SP.
5. Before a subprogram is executed, the contents of any registers that the subprogram accesses need to be saved by pushing them onto the stack.
6. When the subprogram has completed, the register values that were saved on the stack should be restored, in reverse order.
7. Local variable space must be deallocated. This can be done by adding the appropriate value to SP. However, a less error-prone way to deallocate variables is to move the value in the base pointer into the stack pointer.

8. Right before returning, the base pointer value must be restored.
9. Executing a RET instruction terminates the subprogram and returns control to the calling code.
10. When the subprogram returns (to the instruction immediately following the CALL), the programmer should remove the parameters from the stack. The RET instruction pops the return address, but the programmer must explicitly remove any parameters placed on the stack before the call.

6.3   Review Questions

1. Given the following code, what values would be contained in the AX register and memory locations x and y after execution of the code segment is complete?

```
X   DW      1234h
Y   DW      5678h
    ...
    push   X
    mov    AX, 4321h
    push   AX
    push   Y
    pop    AX
    pop    X
    pop    Y
```

2. Trace the following and show the final values in the AX, BX, CX, and DX registers.

```
mov    AX,   10
mov    BX,   8
push   AX
push   BX
add    AX,   6
push   AX
sub    BX,   4
push   BX
pop    AX
pop    BX
pop    CX
pop    DX
```

3. Suppose we execute the following code (assuming a small model of memory):

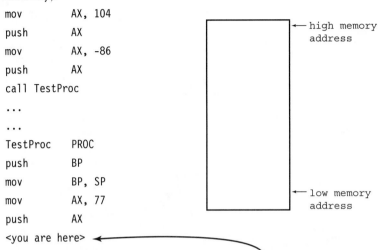

```
mov       AX, 104
push      AX
mov       AX, -86
push      AX
call TestProc
...
...
TestProc  PROC
push      BP
mov       BP, SP
mov       AX, 77
push      AX
<you are here>
```

Draw a picture of what the stack looks like at this point. Also show where SP is pointing.

6.4 Programming Assignments

1. Write a program that uses a procedure to double a number. Pass the value to be doubled in the AX register and place the doubled value in DX. Be sure to save any registers (other than DX) that the procedure modifies.

2. Write a subprogram called PutString that prints the characters pointed at by ES:DI. Print all characters in the string except the terminating byte. Be sure your procedure saves any registers it modifies.

3. Write a procedure called Fib which, when given a value n, produces the nth Fibonacci number. Assume the procedure uses the value found in AX as n, and places the result in DX.

Chapter 7

Input/Output

Up to this point, we have limited I/O in our programs to strings. There is a good reason for this—I/O is a very difficult and confusing topic. Numeric input and output is particularly difficult. The main reason is that *all* input and output is assumed to be ASCII. Therefore, if you wish to output an integer value, you must first convert it to an equivalent ASCII string before it can be output. To input numeric values, they are first input as ASCII strings and are then converted into the corresponding numeric value. Most high-level languages provide routines for numeric input and output, for both integer and floating point values. Since assembly does not, the programmer must code procedures to perform numeric I/O.

Most programmers have libraries of macros or subroutines to perform I/O tasks. A **macro** is a "nickname" for a sequence of other statements. When the assembler sees a macro name, it substitutes the statements in the macro for the macro name (this is called expanding the macro). We do not cover macros in this supplement.

If the I/O routines are subroutines, they are invoked with the CALL statement as we have seen. Your instructor may have some very nice I/O libraries that you can use. However, developing these libraries is beyond the scope of this supplement. Therefore, we show code for simple input and output of characters, strings, and unsigned integers.

7.1   Character and String Output

We have already seen how to output a string, so we begin our discussion with a quick review. We saw previously that output requires using DOS interrupts (INT 21h) with a specific numeric value placed into AH to invoke the correct function. Since a character can be thought of as a string of length 1, we combine these two under one heading. The effective address of the string to be printed must be placed in DX. Then we use the DOS call to display a string:

```
mov   DX, offset Msg    ; DX must contain offset of string
mov   AH, 09h           ; 09h is the DOS code to output a string
int   21h
```

Note that in the above code, we could also place the address of our message in DX by using:

```
lea   DX, Msg
```

Remember, your string must end with a $ for this call to work. If you want to output a single character, you can use the DOS call 2h as follows:

```
mov   DL, Char    ; DL must contain the character to print
mov   AH, 2h      ; 2h is the DOS code to display a char
int   21h         ; Character displayed at cursor position
```

We note that there are many additional input functions that can be used. We do not cover them in this supplement.

7.2   Character Input

The code below shows how to input one single character. No carriage return (Enter) is required after the character is entered. DOS function 01h returns the next character in the keyboard buffer, waiting if necessary. The character is echoed on the screen as well as stored in AL. If a control character is entered, AL will contain 0.

```
mov   AH, 01h     ; 01h is the DOS code to get a character
int   21h         ; The character is put into AL by default
mov   Char, AL    ; Copy character into Char
```

7.3   String Input

We can think of a string as a sequence of characters. Therefore, we can use a loop to repeat the INT 21h instruction and a carriage return (0Dh) to terminate the loop. Assuming we wish to store the string in the variable MyString (be sure MyString is declared large enough to hold the string you input), the code might appear as follows:

```
        mov     DI,offset MyString
        mov     AH,01h
Top:    INT     21H         ; Get a character
        cmp     AL,0Dh      ; Are we at the end of the input?
        je      Done
        mov     [DI],AL     ; Copy character to MyString
        inc     DI          ; Increment pointer in MyString
        jmp     Top         ; Go get next character
Done:   mov     AX, '$'     ; Move the string terminator into AX
        mov     [DI],AX     ;   and then append to string
```

It's a good idea to terminate the string with a '$' so if we output the string, it will output correctly. If you want the string to have a carriage return and line feed, you should insert 10 and 13 before the '$'.

We have another method to input strings. The DOS function 0Ah reads a given number of characters from standard input and puts them into a buffer. Input is terminated when the Enter key is pressed. This function automatically puts 13 (the Enter key) into the buffer.

The 0Ah function requires the offset address of the buffer to be placed in DX. The *first* byte of the buffer must contain the maximum number of characters (including the final carriage return) allowed to be put into the buffer. The *second* byte of this buffer is used to store the actual number of characters that are read into the buffer. Thus, the string to be input is actually stored starting at the *third* byte of the buffer. This implies the buffer must be 3 bytes longer than the maximum length allowed for the string (one byte each for the maximum length, the actual number of characters read, and the carriage return). If a user attempts to input more characters than allowed by the maximum, the keyboard will beep and Enter will be the only allowable key at that point. The DOS call automatically puts a carriage return at the end of the string.

```
Prompt      DB 'Enter a string: ',13,10,$
Buffer      LABEL BYTE      ; Start of string
MaxLength   DB 20           ; Store the max length of string
```

```
ActLength  DB ?              ; Store the actual length of string
MyString   DB 20 DUP(' ')
   ...
   mov     AH,09h            ; Print the input prompt
   mov     DX,offset Prompt
   int     21h
   mov     AH,0Ah            ; Read keyboard input string
   mov     DX,offset Buffer
   int     21h
```

LABEL (in the data declaration) is a directive that causes alignment on a byte boundary. This statement is used to assign a name (Buffer) to the list that follows (including MaxLength, ActLength, and MyString). LABEL takes up no space, so in reality, Buffer and MaxLength refer to the same memory location. This is useful since the Buffer consists of three separate parts. The INT operation waits for the user to type in characters, checking to be sure the user does not exceed the maximum number. This function echos each of the characters as they are entered. When the user presses the Enter key, the character 0Dh is appended to the string (but this is not counted in the actual length). The actual length is stored as the second byte of the buffer, or ActLength in the above code.

7.4   Numeric Input and Output

Numeric input and output is very difficult for the beginning assembly language programmer. Remember, all input and output is ASCII. Numeric input must be read in as ASCII and converted to the corresponding numeric equivalent. The reverse process must be performed to output a numeric value.

Input is more difficult if we opt to check for signs, spaces, and illegal characters. Many existing I/O libraries have very nice routines to check input strings for different characters and convert them to numeric values. We provide simple routines that do little error checking and allow only unsigned integer values to be input. The routines for floating point input and output are very complicated and are not covered in this supplement.

Below we present code to read characters from the keyboard, one at a time, and convert these characters to an unsigned numeric value. It is standard for input and output routines to be procedures or macros. We have set ours up as procedures. The procedure, GetDec, reads from the keyboard, one character at a time, and saves the final decimal value in BX:

```
.DATA
Error  DB  'Illegal digit entered.', 13, 10, '$'
```

```
Prompt DB  'Please enter a decimal value.', 13, 10, '$'
Digit   DW 0
Num1    DW 0
Num2    DW 0
...

GetDec PROC
; This procedure reads characters from the keyboard and
;   converts to an unsigned decimal value stored in BX

     push AX          ; Save registers that procedure modifies
     push CX
     push DX

     mov Digit,0
     mov BX,0         ; Initialize the running total
start:
     mov AH,09h
     mov DX, offset Prompt
     int 21h          ; Prompt for input

nextDigit:
     mov AH,01h
     int 21h          ; Read one character

     cmp AL,0Dh
     je Done          ; If we read Enter, we are done

     ;; valid characters include the characters '0' thru '9'
     ;;   or ASCII 48 thru 57 (30 thru 39 in hex)
     cmp AL,30h       ; Check the range of characters
     jb  BadChar
     cmp AL,39h
     ja  BadChar

     call ConvertInt   ; If valid character, convert
     jmp nextDigit     ; Read the next character

BadChar:
     mov AH,09h
     mov DX,offset Error
     int 21h              ; Print error message and start over

     jmp start

Done:
     pop DX               ; Restore registers
     pop CX
```

```
        pop AX
        ret
GetDec ENDP                ; Final value stored in BX

ConvertInt PROC            ; Multiply previous digit by 10
        mov digit, BX      ;    and add new digit
        mov DX, 0
        mov CX, 10
Times10:
        add DX, BX
        loop Times10
        mov BX, DX
        sub AL, 30h        ; Convert from ASCII to decimal value
        add BL, AL
        mov digit, BX

        ret
ConvertInt ENDP
```

If you needed to input two integer variables, say Num1 and Num2, this could be done as follows:

```
call GetDec
mov  Num1, BX
call GetDec
mov  Num2, BX
```

Alternately, you could read in an entire string and then convert the string to its decimal equivalent:

```
.DATA
IntStr    LABEL BYTE       ; Start of string
MaxLength DB 20            ; Store the max length of string
ActLength DB ?             ; Store the actual length of string
TheString DB 20 DUP(?)
CrLf      DB 13, 10, '$'   ; Carriage return, line feed
   ...

ReadInt    PROC            ; Read an integer into the AX register

    push BX                ; Save all registers modified in
                           ;    procedure

    push CX
    push DX
    push SI
```

```
        mov     AH,0Ah          ; Read in string from keyboard
        lea     DX,IntStr
        int     21h

        mov     CL,ActLength    ; Get actual length of string
        mov     CH,0
        mov     BX,0            ; Initialize digit pointer
        mov     AX,0            ; Initialize running total
        mov     SI,10           ; Multiply by 10 for decimal conversion
MultLoop:
        mul     SI              ; Move total one place to the left
        mov     DH,0
        mov     DL,[BX+TheString]    ; Get next digit
        sub     DL,48           ; Convert ASCII to integer value
        add     AX,DX           ; Add digit to total
        inc     BX              ; Increment digit pointer
        loop MultLoop           ; Loop through all characters (use CX)

        push    AX              ; Save total decimal value
        mov     AH,09h          ; Output carriage return/linefeed
        lea     DX,CrLf
        int     21h
        pop     AX              ; Restore total after output

        pop     SI              ; Restore registers
        pop     DX
        pop     CX
        pop     BX

        ret

ReadInt ENDP
```

The LABEL directive in the above code, used with the BYTE attribute, simply aligns on a byte boundary.

Here is a comparable procedure that prints an unsigned integer. The integer value must first be converted to ASCII; then we simply print the ASCII string.

```
PrintInt  PROC                ; Outputs the integer in the AX register

;; Since PrintInt, and not the main program, needs the string
;;  info we declare it in the procedure here
;; Note that we must first reenter the DATA section

.DATA                         ; Reenter the data section
IntStr      LABEL BYTE        ; Start of string
MaxLength   DB 20             ; Store the max length of string
ActLength   DB ?              ; Store the actual length of string
```

```
TheString DB 25 DUP (?)
CrLf     DB 13, 10, '$'        ; Carriage return, line feed

;; We must now reenter the code section
.CODE                          ; Reenter the code section
    push AX                    ; Save all registers procedure modifies
    push BX
    push CX
    push DX
    push SI

    mov  BX,10                 ; We'll divide by 10 now
    mov  SI,0                  ; Initialize digit pointer
DivLoop:
    mov  DX,0                  ; Zero out remainder
    div  BX                    ; Divide by 10
    push DX                    ; Save remainder
    inc  SI                    ; Increment digit counter
    cmp  AX,0                  ; Continue division?
    jne  DivLoop

    mov  CX,SI                 ; Set digit counter
    mov  BX,0                  ; Initialize position counter
ChangeToAscii:
    pop  AX                    ; Get last digit
    add  AL,48                 ; Convert digit to ASCII
    mov  [TheString+BX],AL     ; Append digit to string
    inc  BX                    ; Increment position pointer
    loop ChangeToAscii
    mov  [TheString+BX],'$'    ; Append end-of-string marker

    mov  AH,09h                ; Output integer as string
    lea  DX,TheString
    int  21h

    mov  AH,09h                ; Output carriage return/linefeed
    lea  DX,CrLf
    int  21h

    pop  SI                    ; Restore registers
    pop  DX
    pop  CX
    pop  BX
    pop  AX

    ret
PrintInt ENDP
```

If you use input or output procedures from an existing library, you should be very careful to note what the procedures expect (preconditions) and what they provide (postconditions). For example, the procedure may expect a certain value to be loaded into the AX register before it is called. An output procedure may or may not include a carriage return and line feed. Be sure you know exactly what the procedures do and how to call them before using them.

7.5   Review Questions

1. What is printed by the following snippet of code?

```
Msg  DB 'Enter a string: ',13,10,$

    mov      DX, offset Msg
    mov      AH, 09h
    int      21h
    mov      DL, Msg
    mov      DL, Char
    mov      AH, 2h
    int      21h
```

2. Explain why numeric input and output is so difficult.

7.6   Programming Assignments

1. Write a program to print your name and age to the screen.
2. Write a program to prompt for four grades. Assume the last grade is an exam and counts twice as much as the others. Display the sum (including the last grade twice) and the average.
3. Write a program to accept a positive integer value n that will print the nth Fibonacci number.
4. The formula for converting a Fahrenheit to a Celsius temperature is: $C = (5/9) \times (F - 32)$. Write a program to prompt for a Fahrenheit temperature and display the corresponding Celsius temperature. Since we only know how to deal with integers, your program should give the integer to which the fractional answer would round. Do *not* divide 5 by 9 first (or you will get zero!).
5. The greatest common divisor (GCD) of two integers is the largest positive integer that divides both evenly. Thus, GCD(100,240) = 20, GCD(34,27) = 1, and GCD(0,14) = 14. Write a subprogram

GCD(*M*,*N*), where *M* and *N* are both integers > 0, without using division. You can use the following loop:

```
while (M≠N) do
  if (N>M) then
    N = N - M
  else
    M = M - N
  endif
endwhile
GCD = N
```

Write a program that calls GCD, assuming *M* and *N* are in AX and BX respectively.

6. Write a program to implement selection sort. Your program should allow the user to input up to 25 word-size unsigned numbers, sort them into increasing order, and print them out in sorted order. Use a procedure to perform the sort. The procedure should use two parameters: the address of the array to be sorted, and the number of elements to be sorted. Use the BX register for the address of the array and the AX register for the number of elements to be sorted.

7. Write a program that prompts the user to enter two strings. If the first string is embedded in the second, the program should report the position of the character in the second string at which the first string appears. If the first string appears multiple times, all instances should be reported. If the first string is *not* replicated in the second, the program should say so. Be careful about overlap!

8. Write a program that accepts a string of up to 20 characters and an integer *n* from the user, and then encrypts the string by shifting the letters *n* units to the "right." For example, if *n* = 4, then A changes to E, S changes to W, and X changes to B. At the end of the alphabet, you will need to "wrap around." You may assume *n* will be less than or equal to 25, and all characters will be in upper case. The program should then display the new string and give the user the option of encrypting another one. Use a procedure to perform the encryption. For additional credit, you can also write a decryption procedure.

9. Write a program to convert an unsigned binary number into printed decimal form (ASCII). Declare the binary number in the DATA section as a 16-bit word (do not input the value). Test your program by using different values for your binary number. Label the output appropriately.

10. Write a program to read in an unsigned decimal number from the keyboard and print the same number in hexadecimal. Your

program should continue to accept numbers from the keyboard until the user enters a zero. You may assume the integer requires no more than 16 bits.

11. Write a program that accepts an arbitrary number of integers and uses a procedure to find the minimum and maximum values. Use the stack to pass values to the procedure.

12. Write a program that uses procedures to input and output signed integers.

Chapter 8

Further Reading

This supplement has provided a brief introduction and overview to Intel assembly language programming. After successfully completing the problems we have presented, you should have a good start on assembly language programming. You will by no means, however, be an expert. There are many advanced topics we did not cover. If you are interested in further study, we suggest the following books:

- *Introduction to 80x86 Assembly Language and Computer Architecture* by Richard Detmer, Jones and Bartlett, 2001
- *Assembly Language for the IBM PC Family* by William Jones, Scott Jones Publishers, 2000
- *IBM PC Assembly Language and Programming* by Peter Abel, 5th Edition, Prentice Hall, 2001
- *Assembly Language for Intel-Based Computers* by Kip R. Irvine, 4th Edition, Prentice Hall, 2002
- *The Art of Assembly Language* by Randall Hyde, No Starch Press, 2003
- *Assembly Language Step-by-Step* by Jeff Duntemann, John Wiley and Sons, 1992
- *Revolutionary Guide to Assembly Language* by Vitaly Maljugin, et al., Wrox Press, 1993

Appendix

Addressing Modes

Immediate

```
OPCODE     <Operand>, <Int>
```

Example: MOV AX, 03Ah

Direct

```
OPCODE     <Memory Address>, <Int or Reg>
OPCODE     <Reg>, <Memory Address>
```

Example: MOV AX, 03Ah

Register

The operand to be used is contained in a register.

```
OPCODE     <Reg>, <Reg or Memory>
```

Example: Add AX, X

Indirect (or Register Indirect)

The address of one operand is stored in BX, SI, or DI. DS is the assumed segment and may be overridden.

```
OPCODE     <Seg:>[Reg], <Int or Reg>
OPCODE     <Reg>, <Seg:>[Reg]
```

Example: MOV ES:[BX], 01Bh

Based-displacement (or Based Relative)

Either of the base register offset pairs, DS:BX or SS:BP, determines the effective address of an operand. These segments may be overridden.

```
OPCODE     <Seg:>[Reg], <Int or Reg>
OPCODE     <Reg>, <Seg:>[Reg]
```

Example: MOV AX, [BP]+9

Base-Index (or Based Indexed)

Register BX or BP holds the base address, and DI or SI supplies the index. Either base register can be combined with either index register. DS is the default segment and can be overridden.

```
OPCODE     <Seg:>[Base reg][Index Reg]
OPCODE     <Reg>, <Seg:> [Base reg][Index Reg]
```

Example: MOV AX, SS:[BX][SI]

Base-Index-with-displacement

Register BX or BP holds the base address, and DI or SI supplies the index, with an additional displacement. Either base register can be combined with either index register. DS is the default segment and can be overridden.

```
OPCODE     <Seg:>[Base reg][Index Reg], <Int or Reg>
OPCODE     <Reg>, <Seg:> [Base reg][Index Reg]
```

Example: MOV AX, SS:[BX][SI]+14

Data Movement Instructions

Load Effective Address (LEA)

```
LEA        <register>, MemoryVariable
```
Places the address of MemoryVariable into the specified register.
Equivalently:
```
MOV <register>, OFFSET MemoryVariable
```

Move (MOV)

```
MOV        <destination>, <source>
```
Places a copy of <source> in <destination>.

Exchange (XCHG)

```
XCHG <destination>, <source>
```
Exchanges the values of <source> and <destination>.

Arithmetic Instructions

Add (ADD)

ADD <destination>, <source>

Adds <source> to <destination>. Result is in <destination>.

Decrement (DEC)

DEC <destination>

Reduces the value of <destination> by 1.

Divide (DIV)

DIV <source>

In unsigned word arithmetic, divides DX:AX by <source>, placing the result in AX. In unsigned byte arithmetic, divides AX by <source>, placing the result in AL.

IDIV <source>

Divides DX:AX, or AX by <source>, placing the signed integer quotient result in AX or DX:AX.

Increment (INC)

INC <destination>

Increases the value of <destination> by 1.

Multiply (MUL)

MUL <source>

In unsigned word arithmetic, multiplies AX by <source>, placing the result in DX:AX. In unsigned byte arithmetic, multiplies AL by <source>, placing the result in AX.

IMUL <source>

Multiplies AX, or AL by <source>, placing the signed product result in AX or DX:AX.

Subtract (SUB)

SUB <destination>, <source>

Subtracts <source> from <destination>. Result is in <destination>.

Control Structures

Unconditional Jump (JMP)

JMP <destination>

Adds the value of <destination> to the value in IP, effectively branching the program to <destination>.

JMP FAR PTR <destination>

Adds the value of the offset <destination> to the value in IP, and replaces CS with the segment in which <destination> is defined.

Note: <destination> must be declared as a FAR LABEL somewhere in the program.

JMP SHORT <destination>

Adds the value of <destination> to the value in IP where <destination> is an 8-bit signed value.

Comparison (CMP)

CMP <destination>, <source>

Any of CF, OF, SF, or ZF may be affected by this operation. The states of these flags are significant for the execution of conditional jump instructions.

Conditional Jump (JA)

JA/JNBE <destination>

Jump when source greater than destination by unsigned comparison (CF = 0 or ZF = 0).

JAE/JNB <destination>

Jump when source greater than or equal to destination (CF = 0) by unsigned comparison.

JB/JNAE <destination>

Jump when source less than destination by unsigned comparison (CF = 1).

JBE/JNA <destination>

Jump when source less than or equal to destination by unsigned comparison (CF = 1 or ZF = 1).

JE/JZ <destination>
Jump if equal (ZF = 1).

JG/JNLE <destination>

Jump when source greater than destination by signed comparison (SF = OF or ZF = 0).

JGE/JNL <destination>

Jump when source greater than or equal to destination by signed comparison (SF = OF).

JL/JNGE <destination>

Jump when source greater than destination by signed comparison (SF ≠ OF).

`JLE/JNG <destination>`
Jump when source less than destination by signed comparison (ZF = 1 and SF ≠ OF).

`JNE/JNZ   <destination>`
Jump if not equal (ZF = 1).

Iteration

`LOOP      <destination>`
Decrement the value in CX and branch to <destination> if CX is nonzero.

`LOOPE/LOOPZ <destination>`
Loop to <destination> only while CX is nonzero and the zero flag is 1.

`LOOPNE/LOOPNZ <destination>`
Loop to <destination> only while CX and the zero flag are both nonzero.

Boolean Operations

`AND <destination>, <source>`
Perform the bitwise AND of <source> and <destination> and place in <destination>.

`OR <destination>, <source>`
Perform the bitwise OR of <source> and <destination> and place in <destination>.

`XOR  <destination>, <source>`
Perform the bitwise XOR of <source> and <destination> and place in <destination>.

Bit Shifting Operations

`RCL <destination>, 1`
`RCL <destination>, CL`
Rotate all bits of <destination> to the left by one position, placing the high-order bit into the carry bit and the carry bit into the low-order bit. To shift by more than one bit, specify the number of bits to shift in CL.

`ROL <destination>, 1`
`ROL <destination>, CL`
Rotate all bits of <destination> to the left by one position, placing the high-order bit into the low-order bit. To shift by more than one bit, specify the number of bits to shift in CL.

```
RCR <destination>, 1
RCR <destination>, CL
```
Rotate all bits of <destination> to the right by one position, placing the low-order bit into the carry bit and the carry bit into the high-order bit. To shift by more than one bit, specify the number of bits to shift in CL.

```
ROR <destination>, 1
ROR <destination>, CL
```
Rotate all bits of <destination> to the right by one position, placing the low-order bit into the high-order bit. To shift by more than one bit, specify the number of bits to shift in CL.

```
SAL <destination>, 1
SAL <destination>, CL
```
Perform arithmetic left shift of <destination> by one place. Same instruction as SHL.

```
SHL/SHR <destination>, 1
SHL/SHR <destination>, CL
```
Shift each bit of <destination> to the left/right one place. Fills rightmost/leftmost bit with 0 and carries the leftmost/rightmost bit into the sign bit. To shift by more than one bit, specify the number of bits to shift in CL.

```
SAR <destination>, 1
SAR <destination>, CL
```
Perform arithmetic left shift right of <destination> by one place. If the sign bit in <destination> is set, it will still be set after the right shift, and propagated to the adjacent bit. The rightmost bit propagates to the carry flag.

Arrays and Strings

```
CLD
```
Clear the direction flag so that a string operation will start at the lowest address. The address pointer will be incremented throughout the operation.

```
LODSB/LODSW <String1>
```
Place the byte or word at address String1 and place it into or AX.

MOVSB/MOVSW <String2>, <String1>
Perform a byte-by-byte, or word-by-word copy of String1 to String2. The addresses of String1 and String2 must be in DS:SI and ES:DI, respectively. CX contains the number of bytes to move. See the REP, CLD, and STD instructions.

REP <string operation>
A prefix that repeats a string operation, such as MOVSB and STOSW, for the number of iterations given in CX.

REPE/REPZ <string operation>
A prefix that repeats a string operation, such as MOVSB and STOSW, until the value in AL (or AX) matches a value in a byte string (or word string).

REPNE/REPNZ <string operation>
A prefix that repeats a string operation, such as MOVSB and STOSW, until the value in AL (or AX) differs from a value in a byte string (or word string).

SCASB/SCASW <String1>
Search String1 for the value contained in AL or AX. Typically used in conjunction with REPE or REPNE.

STD
Set the direction flag so that a string operation will start at the highest address. The address pointer will be decremented throughout the operation.

STOSB/STOSW <String1>
Place the current value of AL or AX into String1.